HOW THE GOVERNMENT CONSPIRED TO "TAKE" BILLIONS FROM A Black Man

LARRY GOLDEN

The Inventor of the "Smartphone"

Written by "*Pro Se*" Larry Golden

CASE STUDY / CONTENT PAGES

FOREWORD

The Government is good at stealing the works of Blacks and/or African Americans; but the Government can't do it alone. To date, the way the Government is successful at stealing the innovations of Blacks and/or African Americans is to have Courts that are supporters of, and enforcers of, systemic and structural racism.

Apple's first smartphone was released in 2007. Apple added GPS to their phones in 2008. Golden's patent(s) disclosure priority date for his communicating, monitoring, detecting, and controlling (CMDC) device, (i.e. smartphone), is November 26, 2004, and includes GPS, internet, CPU, and CBRNE sensors. Three years before Apple released its first smartphone.

Golden filed his first patent on April 5, 2006. Both Golden's USPTO disclosure date (2004) and first application filing date (2006) antedates Apple's release of its first smartphone.

According to Nancy Pelosi ("Government"), "Apple did not invent the Smartphone, the Government did".

"Apple can't get much respect from the government lately. Months after the company fought a tense legal battle with the FBI over iPhone security, the Democratic leader in the U.S. House of Representatives is questioning how much credit Apple should get for creating the iPhone. In comments this week, Rep. Nancy Pelosi (D-Calif.) said "federal research" -- not Steve Jobs or Apple -- invented the iPhone.

"Pelosi made the comments during a hearing on Thursday to help draft the Democratic Party platform, a multi-day event to prepare for the Democratic National Convention in July. While talking about the need for more public-private partnerships to help foster innovation, she held up what appears to be an iPhone 6S Plus (or 6 Plus)" and said:

"Anybody here have a smartphone? In this smartphone, almost everything came from federal investments and research. GPS, created by the military, flatscreens, LLD [sic], digital camera, wireless data compression, research into metal alloys for strength and lightweight, voice recognition -- the list goes on and on.... They say Steve Jobs did a good idea designing it and putting it together. Federal research invented it."

"What Pelosi seems to be saying was that federal funding and research played a key role in many of the underlying technologies within the iPhone, which is true. As just one example, the U.S. military developed GPS technology, which powers much of the location-based data that's fundamental to smartphones today."

Reference
Nancy Pelosi says 'federal research' invented the iPhone, not Steve Jobs. By Pete Pachal on June 10, 2016

Golden agrees in-part and disagrees in-part. Yes, it was the Government who initiated contracts and made awards for the development and assembly of the smartphone, but it was Golden who invented the smartphone. It was Golden who spent fours years convincing the Government [2003-2007] that if they adopt Golden's product grouping strategy and make a request for Golden's communicating, monitoring, detecting, and controlling (CMDC) device [smartphone]; the demand for the device will stimulate the Nation's economy. The development and assembly of the smartphone is described below.

- ***Department of Homeland Security***: For the program's initial phase in 2007, DHS released a call for proposals inviting the private sector to develop a proof of concept for the "*Cell-All Ubiquitous Biological and Chemical Sensing*" project in 2007

(DHS S&T BAA07-10). The ideological underpinning for the Cell-All project is one of neoliberal public–private partnerships, by which industry profits from privileged government contracts. Once mobile phone manufacturers routinely include chemical and other sensors in their devices, users can be compelled or coerced to communicate environmental data as such sharing becomes normalized in technical protocol. Cell-All began in 2010 with the goal of creating dozens of competing viable devices and refining the network capabilities of the system. At this stage, DHS also sought to standardize the data reporting protocols so that data from different devices could be received and processed by a centralized network operations center. HSARPA accelerates this process through direct commercial partnerships, where it funds researchers from both the public and the private sector to develop products that can then be brought to market. Public subsidization of private companies, is rationalized through discourses of efficiency. DHS believe that technology transfer directly to the commercial [sector] is an efficient way to go. In order for the Cell-All public safety sensing and alerting system to be complete, four links must be forged and joined together: the sensor and computing hardware, the sensing application for mobile phones, a centralized server and network operations center, and the end consumer, whether individuals, emergency operations centers, first responders, government agencies, or private companies. The eventual goal of the project is to embed multiple nanoscale sensors (for environmental chemicals, industrial toxins, radiation, and bioagents) directly into mobile phones. During the development of second-generation prototypes, chemical sensors were separated from the phones, allowing for initial market deployment of the sensors through third-party products, such as sleeves, that could be added to existing phones. This use of accessory products is intended to speed up the technology's commercial availability so that people can begin using the Cell-All applications with their current phones before integrated sensors are fully operational and readily available. *Crowdsourcing urban surveillance: The development of homeland security markets for environmental sensor networks.* SciVerse ScienceDirect. Geoforum 49 (2013) 279–288. journal homepage: www.elsevier.com/locate/geoforum.

- ***Rhevision***: A cell phone's camera used to monitor color changes to the camera lens: lenses spot a color related to poison, will trigger an alert system on the cell phone. Rhevision, invented the miniature tunable camera lens, which makes the lenses. *Homeland Security wants to turn your cell phone into a smell phone.* https://www.csmonitor.com/Science/2010/0520/Homeland-Security-wants-to-turn-your-cell-phone-into-a-smell phone#:~:text=The%20U.S.%20Department%20of%20 Homeland%20Security%20%28DHS%29%20is,phones%20and%20alert%20users%20to%20potentially%20deadly%20smells

- *NASA*: The platform, developed using NASA nanotechnology, paved the way for interchangeable smartphone sensors. Li convinced the program manager at DHS that the sensor should be a module attached to the outside of the phone. The modular design paved the way for future smartphone chemical sensors; the line of interchangeable, smartphone-savvy sensors Yu would commercialize. The design for the microprocessor, memory, communication protocol, back-end Web structure, data storage, and cloud technology he developed for NASA and DHS. *Wireless Platform Integrates Sensors with Smartphones.* https://www.techbriefs.com/component/content/article/26213-wireless-platform-integrates-sensors-with-smartphones

- *Seacoast Science*: "I wanted to meet with the founders of Seacoast Science since I learned in late October that the Carlsbad, CA, startup is part of a government-sponsored initiative to embed tiny chemical sensors in cell phones", says Bruce Bigelow. Seacoast's technology is impressive: tiny microchips—about the size of the typeface on a postage stamp—each containing multiple individual sensors, or "chemical capacitors." In its development of chemical sensors for cell phones, Seacoast Science has been working with Qualcomm, the wireless technology giant based in San Diego. *Bigelow, B. (2010, Feb.4). The San Diego Union-Tribune: Seacoast Science Avoids VCs, Finds Other Money to Develop Tiny Chemical Sensors.*

- ***Synkera Technologies***: The widespread use of cell phones could be harnessed with an ability to detect chemical threats and immediately notify authorities. Synkera proposes to develop a unique nanostructured ceramic sensor array for threat detection. This miniature detection system is well suited for integration with cellular and other wireless devices and will enable them to become part of a larger distributed alert network that improves situational awareness for mission personnel. Miniature and Reliable Chemical Sensors for Cell Phones. https://www.sbir.gov/node/1302955

- ***Qualcomm***: HSARPA already is working with NASA, Qualcomm and Rhevision Technology to create the new sensors. Each organization takes different scientific approaches to the problem. According to the Department of Homeland Security (DHS), Qualcomm engineers specialize in the necessary miniaturization and have the knowledge required to move a product to the marketplace. https://www.afcea.org/signal-media/technology/sensor-every-pocket. HSARPA conducted a national search for ideas that was intended to leverage existing technological expertise in the public and private sectors, which led to the creation of six workable first-generation prototypes, including a "form factor phone" developed by Qualcomm: as a Qualcomm representative argued: "Let's take advantage of the 300 million cell phones that are out there today. They're always with us" (Hoffman, 2011) *Crowdsourcing urban surveillance: The development of homeland security markets for* *environmental sensor networks.* SciVerse Science Direct. Geoforum 49 (2013) 279–288. journal page: www.elsevier.com/locate/ geoforum.

- ***Qualcomm*:** Qualcomm's role has been to develop a smartphone app and the associated network software for processing data. When the application is installed, it will ask the user for permission to share sensor readings and location information over the network; then, whenever abnormal chemical levels are detected, the phone will send those data to a network gateway. According to Doug Hoffman, program manager at Qualcomm, the gateway will authenticate the sensor and phone to determine whether they are authorized to be on the network, scrub personal information from the data, assign a temporary identification number to the phone, and then send data to the network operations center (NOC). *Crowdsourcing urban surveillance: The development of homeland security markets for environmental sensor networks.* SciVerse ScienceDirect. Geoforum 49 (2013) 279–288. journal homepage: www.elsevier.com/locate/geoforum.

- ***Qualcomm, Apple, Samsung, and LG*:** S&T pursued what's known as cooperative research and development agreements with four cell phone manufacturers: Qualcomm, LG, Apple, and Samsung. These written agreements, which bring together a private company and a government agency for a specific project, often accelerate the commercialization of technology developed for government purposes. Bill Gates once envisioned a computer on every desk in every home, so Stephen Dennis envisions a chemical sensor in every cell phone in every pocket, purse, or belt holster. *Cell-All: Super Smartphones Sniff Out Suspicious Substances.* https://www.dhs.gov/science-and-technology/cell-all-super-smartphones-sniff-out-suspicious-substances

- ***Google*:** "Smartphone users can download the app from Google Play and, eventually, from Apple's iTunes store, so Cell-All will be operational on all phones using either Google's Android or Apple's iPhone operating systems." *Crowdsourcing urban surveillance: The development of homeland security markets for environmental sensor networks.* SciVerse ScienceDirect. Geoforum 49 (2013) 279–288. journal homepage: www.elsevier.com/ locate/geoforum.

The significant modifications Golden made to the cell phone that are covered in Golden's patent specifications and claimed in twenty-eight (28) independent patent claims and eighteen (18) dependent patent claims of Golden's United States Patents has a USPTO priority date (disclosure document) of November 26, 2004.

INTRODUCTION TO CASE STUDY

This case of "judicial misconduct" in the Northern District of California case of 4:22-cv-05246-RFL is directed at Judge Rita F. Lin of the United States District Court for the Northern District of California, for whom the complainant believes willfully violated Golden's civil rights under statutes 18 U.S.C. § 241 and 18 U.S.C. § 242. Golden is alleging Judge Rita F. Lin conspired against the rights of the complainant and acted under the color of the law to willfully deprive Golden of his Seventh Amendment right to a trial by jury or privilege protected by the United States Constitution or laws of the United States. According to the Civil Rights Division of the Department of Justice:

> 18 U.S.C. § 241. Conspiracy against Rights: Section 241 makes it unlawful for two or more persons to agree to injure, threaten, or intimidate a person [Golden] in the United States in the free exercise or enjoyment of any right or privilege secured by the Constitution or laws of the United States or because of his or her having exercised such a right. Unlike most conspiracy statutes, § 241 does not require, as an element, the commission of an overt act.
>
> 18 U.S.C. § 242. Deprivation of Rights Under Color of Law: This provision makes it a crime for [Judge Rita F. Lin] acting

> under color of law to willfully deprive a person [Golden] of a right or privilege protected by the Constitution or laws of the United States. It is not necessary that the offense be motivated by racial bias or by any other animus. Those prosecuted under the statute include judges, district attorneys, other public officials.

In order to promote the proper administration of justice, Judge Rita F. Lin enjoy absolute immunity from suit. See *Mireles v. Waco*, 502 U.S. 9, 112 S. Ct. 286, 116 L. Ed. 2d 9 (1991); *Boyd v. Biggers*, 31 F.3d 279 (5th Cir.1994). But Judge Rita F. Lin does not escape penalties for "judicial misconduct" and for willfully violating the "code of conduct" for United States judges.

The complainant may overcome Judge Rita F. Lin judicial immunity under certain circumstances. For example, the Supreme Court has recognized two circumstances in which a complainant may overcome Judge Rita F. Lin's immunity: "First, [the] judge is not immune from liability for nonjudicial actions, i.e., actions not taken in the judge's judicial capacity. ... Second, [the] judge is not immune for actions, though judicial in nature, taken in the complete absence of all jurisdiction." *Mireles*, 502 U.S. at 11-12, 112 S. Ct. 286.

In other words, Judge Rita F. Lin was absent of all jurisdiction of the Northern District of California Court when the Judge made it a requirement that the complainant "prove direct infringement under 28 U.S.C. § 1498(a) [government infringement of combining patented combinations—Golden's patented cell phone with the DoD DTRA ATAK software] as a necessary predicate to proving direct infringement under 35 U.S.C. § 271(a). *Zoltek III.*

Judge Rita F. Lin dismissed Golden's case because Golden refuse to deny or reject the opinion of the Federal Circuit in *Golden v. Google, LLC* CAFC Case No. 22-1267, that his patented combinations more likely than not prove literal infringement and/or infringement under the doctrine of equivalents. [28 U.S.C. § 271(a)].

In *Zoltek V*, the appellate court emphasized that § 1498(a) is "its own independent cause of action" with three elements to trigger government liability: (1) the invention must be claimed in a patent; (2) it must be "used or manufactured by or for the United States," meaning each limitation of the claims must be present in the accused product or process; and (3) the "use or manufacture" of the patented invention must be done without license or lawful right—i.e., "use of an invention that, if done by a private party, would directly infringe the patent." 672 F.3d at 1321, 1323.

Therefore again, Judge Rita F. Lin adjudicated Golden's case in a way that she knew it was outside the Northern District of California Court jurisdiction. Consequently, any decisions made by Judge Rita F. Lin are considered moot and cannot be a decision based on the merits of the case, because Judge Rita F. Lin adjudicated the case in the wrong jurisdiction.

Because Judge Rita F. Lin allegedly knew the Northern District of California Court lack jurisdiction, the Court is barred from deciding Golden's suit under 28 U.S.C. § 1498(a) [government infringement]. Because of race, Judge Lin deprived Golden of his constitutional right to a trial by jury [U.S. CONST' amend. VII]; deprived Golden of his property without due process of law and without paying just compensation [U.S. CONST' amend. V]; knowingly violated Golden's civil rights under 42 U.S.C. § 1983, 18 U.S.C. §§ 241 & 242; and joined as a co-conspirator an already established conspiracy of judicial systemic and structural racism.

CHAPTER ONE

JUDGE RITA F. LIN IS A CO-CONSPIRATOR IN AN ALREADY ESTABLISHED JUDICIAL SYSTEM OF "SYSTEMIC AND STRUCTURAL RACISM"

Considering the evidence presented in this complaint, it is easy to say Judge Rita F. Lin is bias in favor of Google and a co-conspirator who joined an already established conspiracy to ensure Blacks and/or African Americans are not compensated for their work.

"Systemic racism is said to occur when racially unequal opportunities and outcomes are inbuilt or intrinsic to the operation of a society's structures. Simply put, systemic racism refers to the processes and outcomes of racial inequality and inequity in life opportunities and treatment. Systemic racism permeates a society's (a) institutional structures (practices, policies, climate), (b) social structures (state/federal programs, laws, culture), (c) individual mental structures (e.g., learning, memory, attitudes, beliefs, values), and (d) everyday interaction patterns (norms, scripts, habits)." (Jones, 1971)

"Systemic racism not only operates at multiple levels; it can emerge with or without animus or intention to harm and with or without awareness of its existence. Its power derives from it being integrated into a unified system of racial differentiation and discrimination that creates, governs, and adjudicates opportunities and outcomes across generations. Racism represents the biases of the powerful" (Jones, 1971) Jones JM. The political dimensions of black liberation. The Black Scholar. 1971;3(1):67–75).

"Intellectual property--specifically patents and copyrights--is expressly protected by the U.S. Constitution. The evolution of intellectual property law, concurrent with our country's laws, has been laced with both overt and covert elements of racism. Not only was the Dred Scott decision used to bar Blacks from the personhood required to qualify for patent protection, but the U.S. Patent Office also declared that enslaved Blacks could not hold patents. As the "promotion of progress," as mandated by the Constitution, became embedded in our national psyche, our country is charged with advancing that goal." (Iams, 2023)

Sophia Cortez Iams. (01 August 2023). Race, Racism, and the Law. "*Patently Biased: A Discussion of Historical and Systemic Causes of Racial Disparity in Patent Law*". Retrieved from: https://racism.org/articles/basic-needs/propertyland/218-intellectual-property/11443-patently-biased

Dred Scott v. Sandford, decided by the U.S. Supreme Court on March 6, 1857, declared that Black people, whether free or enslaved, could not be American citizens and were thus constitutionally unable to sue for citizenship in the federal courts. The Court's majority opinion also declared that the 1820 Missouri Compromise was unconstitutional and that the U.S. Congress could not prohibit enslavement in the U.S. territories that had not attained statehood.

Why would the patent office of the North be so discriminatory against black people during the Civil War? Joseph Holt, head of the Patent Office at the time, was from Kentucky and interpreted *Dredd Scott* to mean that a free black person who had escaped to the North didn't have the right to patent his invention. Holt also denied free black men from northern states the same right, despite objections from northern senators like Charles Sumner of Massachusetts.

Among constitutional scholars, *Scott v. Sandford* is widely considered the worst decision ever rendered by the Supreme Court. It has been cited in particular as the most egregious example in the Supreme Court's history of wrongly imposing a judicial solution on a political problem. A later chief justice, Charles Evans Hughes, famously characterized the decision as the court's great "self-inflicted wound."

In the Supreme Court, *Return Mail, Inc. v. United States Postal Service,* 868 F. 3d 1350, BREYER, J., filed a dissenting opinion, in which GINSBURG and KAGAN, JJ., joined. The Court ruled that Government agencies are not "persons" authorized to petition the PTAB for inter partes review to invalidate a patent. But Justice Breyer writes in his dissenting opinion:

> "[w]hen, for example, the Department of Homeland Security recently instituted a research initiative to equip cell phones with hazardous-materials sensors in order to mitigate the risk of terrorist attacks, it faced an infringement lawsuit that threatened to interfere with the project. See *Golden v. United States,* 129 Fed. Cl. 630 (2016); ...

Golden has petition for writ in three different cases only to be denied. The Supreme Court can publicly enter Golden's case into an unrelated case *Return Mail* only to say 'Golden should have had his patents taken by the unauthorized government agencies', because Golden will never get the chance, as a Black and/or African American inventor, to correct the record and explain to the Court that it was Golden who spent four years sharing with DHS; before the DHS decided in 2008 to give seven white-owned companies his intellectual property to develop. Chart follows:

THE JUSTICES OF THE UNITED STATES SUPREME COURT ARE ALLEGED TO BE CO-CONSPIRATORS IN AN ALREADY ESTABLISHED CONSPIRACY

U.S. Supreme Court: Docket for 23-904. Title: Larry Golden, Petitioner v. United States ***Petition Denied*** March 25, 2024 Larry Golden, Petitioner United States Court of Appeals for the Federal Circuit Petition for a writ of certiorari filed. Party name: Larry Golden
U.S. Supreme Court: Docket for 23-740. Title: Larry Golden, Petitioner v. Qualcomm, Inc. ***Petition Denied*** March 18, 2024 Larry Golden, Petitioner

United States Court of Appeals for the Federal Circuit Petition for a writ of certiorari filed. Party name: Larry Golden
U.S. Supreme Court: Docket for 23-1001. Title: Larry Golden, Petitioner v. Samsung Electronics America, Inc. ***Petition Denied*** April 22, 2024 Larry Golden, Petitioner United States Court of Appeals for the Federal Circuit Petition for a writ of certiorari filed. Party name: Larry Golden

THE "CONSPIRACY" FORMED BETWEEN THE JUDGES OF THE APPELLATE COURTS, DISTRICT COURTS, AND THE COURT OF FEDERAL CLAIMS

Party Name	Case Number	Case Title	Court	Filed - Closed
Larry Golden	2023cvpri02120	Golden v. Samsung Electronics America, Inc.	U.S. Court Of Appeals, Federal Circuit	07/07/2023 - 02/12/2024
Larry Golden	2018cvus01942	Golden v. US	U.S. Court Of Appeals, Federal Circuit	05/10/2018 - 08/01/2018
Larry Golden	2019and00100	Golden In re: Golden	U.S. Court Of Appeals, Federal Circuit	10/03/2018 - 11/05/2018
Larry Golden	2019cvus02134	Golden v. US	U.S. Court Of Appeals, Federal Circuit	07/12/2019 - 04/10/2020
Larry Golden	2019cvus02135	Golden v. US	U.S. Court Of Appeals, Federal Circuit	07/12/2019 - 09/13/2019
Larry Golden	2020cvpri01508	Golden v. Apple Inc.	U.S. Court Of Appeals, Federal Circuit	02/25/2020 - 09/03/2020

Larry Golden	2022cvus01196	Golden v. US	U.S. Court Of Appeals, Federal Circuit	11/29/2021 - 09/08/2022
Larry Golden	2022cvpri01229	Golden v. Apple Inc.	U.S. Court Of Appeals, Federal Circuit	12/07/2021 - 09/08/2022
Larry Golden	2022cvpri01267	Golden v. Google LLC	U.S. Court Of Appeals, Federal Circuit	12/16/2021 - 09/08/2022
Larry Golden	2023cvpri01161	Golden v. Apple Inc.	U.S. Court Of Appeals, Federal Circuit	01/18/2022 - 05/12/2023
Larry Golden	2023cvpri01257	Golden v. Intel Corporation	U.S. Court Of Appeals, Federal Circuit	12/16/2022 - 05/05/2023
Larry Golden	2023cvpri01818	Golden v. Qualcomm Incorporated	U.S. Court Of Appeals, Federal Circuit	04/28/2023 - 10/10/2023
Larry Golden	2023cvus02139	Golden v. US	U.S. Court Of Appeals, Federal Circuit	07/11/2023 - 12/15/2023
Larry Golden	3:2022cv05246	Golden v. Google LLC	California Northern District Court	09/14/2022 - 04/03/2024
Larry Golden	4:2022cv03283	Golden v. Qualcomm, Inc	California Northern District Court	06/06/2022 - 03/15/2023
Larry Golden	5:2022cv03828	Golden v. Intel Corporation	California Northern District Court	06/28/2022 - 11/22/2022
Larry Golden	3:2022cv04152	Golden v. Apple Inc.	California Northern District Court	07/15/2022 - 10/20/2022
Larry Golden	3:2023cv00048	Golden v. Samsung	California Northern District Court	01/05/2023 - 06/08/2023

		Electronics America, Inc.		
Larry Golden	1:2013cv00307	Golden v. USA	U.S. Court of Federal Claims	05/01/2013 - 11/10/2021
Larry Golden	1:2019cv00104	Golden v. USA	U.S. Court of Federal Claims	01/17/2019 - 05/15/2019
Larry Golden	1:2023cv00185	Golden v. USA	U.S. Court of Federal Claims	02/07/2023 - 05/31/2023
Larry Golden	1:2023cv00811	Golden v. USA	U.S. Court of Federal Claims	05/31/2023 - 04/24/2024
Larry Golden	6:2021cv00244	Golden v. Google LLC	South Carolina District Court	01/26/2021 - 04/19/2023
Larry Golden	6:2019cv02557	Golden v. Apple Inc. et al	South Carolina District Court	09/11/2019 - 01/27/2020
Larry Golden	6:2020cv02270	Golden v. Apple Inc. et al	South Carolina District Court	06/16/2020 - 09/20/2021
Larry Golden	6:2020cv04353	Golden v. Apple Inc. et al	South Carolina District Court	12/16/2020 - 12/01/2021

The chart above is representative of the number of times Golden, a Black and/or African American, have filed cases in the Supreme Court, the Appellate Courts, the District Court, and the Court of Federal Claims and has never gotten pass the pleading stage, over the past ten years.

The chart above is also illustrative of the number of times Golden, a Black and/or African American, have been deprived "due process of law" and a jury trial as guaranteed by the Seventh Amendment of the United States Constitution.

In this current case, *Larry Golden v. Google LLC*, NDC Case 3:22-cv-05246-RFL Order Granting Motion to Dismiss… Dkt. 68; Filed 04/03/24. Judge Rita F. Lin confirmed to all the other co-conspirators that she was onboard with the purpose and intent of the conspiracy and that she was not going to be the one to break ranks.

"The motion to dismiss is GRANTED WITHOUT LEAVE TO AMEND. This ruling assumes the reader is familiar with the facts, the applicable legal standard, and the arguments made by the parties" … "This case is one of several patent infringement cases that Golden has filed against Google and other defendants. See *Golden v. Samsung Elecs. Am., Inc.*, No. 23-CV-00048-WHO, 2023 WL 3919466 (N.D. Cal. June 8, 2023), aff'd, No. 2023-2120, 2024 WL 539973 (Fed. Cir. Feb. 12, 2024) (***describing Golden's litigation history over the past ten years in multiple jurisdictions***)" … "Leave to amend may be denied for "repeated failure to cure deficiencies by previous amendment." *Abagninin v. AMVAC Chem. Corp.*, 545 F.3d 733, 742 (9th Cir. 2008)." … "The flaws in the FAC are the same as those identified in the order dismissing Golden's original complaint. As Golden was already granted leave to amend once in this case but was unable to correct the deficiencies, further leave to amend would be futile."

"Furthermore, ***Golden has had multiple suits with similar allegations dismissed, some as frivolous.*** See, e.g., *Golden v. Samsung Elecs. Am., Inc.*, No. 23-CV-00048-WHO, 2023 WL 3919466 (N.D. Cal. June 8,

2023), aff'd, No. 2023-2120, 2024 WL 539973 (Fed. Cir. Feb. 12, 2024); *Golden v. Qualcomm, Inc.*, No. 22-CV-03283-HSG, 2023 WL 2530857 (N.D. Cal. Mar. 15, 2023) *Golden v. Apple Inc.*, No. 20-cv-04353-JD-KFM, 2021 WL 5074739 (D.S.C. Nov. 2, 2021) (dismissing complaint as "frivolous"); *Golden v. Apple Inc.,* No. 20-cv-02270-JD-KFM, 2021 WL 4260782 (D.S.C. Sept. 20, 2021) (dismissing complaint as "frivolous")."

Judge Rita F. Lin qualified herself as a co-conspirator to the already established conspiracy form and administered by the Judges, defendants, and defendants' attorneys of previous cases filed by Golden. The conspiracy is to never allow Golden's case to ever get pass the pleading stage, no matter what evidence Golden submits to support his case at the pleading stage, and to never allow the facts of Golden's case to ever be heard by a jury of his peers. Judge Rita F. Lin is in violation of 18 U.S.C. § 241. Conspiracy against Rights:

> "Section 241 makes it unlawful for two or more persons to agree to injure, threaten, or intimidate a person [Golden] in the United States in the free exercise or enjoyment of any right or privilege secured by the Constitution or laws of the United States or because of his or her having exercised such a right. Unlike most conspiracy statutes, § 241 does not require, as an element, the commission of an overt act."

Judge Rita F. Lin acknowledges "[t]his case is one of several patent infringement cases that Golden has filed against Google. If the two cases filed (*Golden v. Google LLC,* SCDC No. 6:2021cv00244 and *Golden v. Google LLC,* N.D.Cal. No.4:22-cv-05246-RFL) qualifies as several, then so be it. Judge Rita F. Lin supports the theory of the conspiracy—use whatever means necessary to ensure Golden, a Black and/or African American—do not proceed beyond the pleading stage, even if it means classifying Golden's case as too unbelievable or too fantastical (i.e., "frivolous").

The co-conspirator Judge Rita F. Lin is especially fascinated in applying "frivolous" to Golden's patented inventions because "[t]here have been numerous expressly racially biased laws promulgated throughout the United States. Among the earliest was the "Three-Fifths Compromise" established in 1787 which treated each enslaved African as only three-fifths of a person for representation in the House of Delegates. In 1857, the Supreme Court essentially held that Blacks were not citizens and thus were not afforded protection under the Constitution in their infamous *Dred Scott v. Sandford* decision."

The "Three-Fifths Compromise" is said to have been nullified in the adoption of the 13th and 14th Amendments, but the spirit of the compromise lives on in a judicial system of "systemic and structural" racism, and the co-conspirator Judge Rita F. Lin is at the heart of it all.

The original case *Golden v. Google LLC*, SCDC No. 6:2021cv00244 was filed in the South Carolina District Court on 01/26/2021. The case was dismissed as being "frivolous". Golden appealed the case to the U.S. Court of Appeals for the Federal Circuit.

The Federal Circuit in *Golden v. Google LLC* Case No. 22-1267 disclosed in "Discussion" that the Circuit reviewed the case "under the pleading standards set forth in *Bell Atlantic Corp. v. Twombly,* 550 U.S. 544 (2007), and *Ashcroft v. Iqbal,* 556 U.S. 662 (2009), [a court must dismiss a complaint if it fails to allege "enough facts to state a claim to relief that is plausible on its face]." *Twombly,* 550 U.S. at 570; and, "plaintiff must allege facts that give rise to "more than a sheer possibility that a defendant has acted unlawfully." *Iqbal,* 556 U.S. at 678 (citation omitted)

The Federal Circuit in *Golden v. Google LLC* Case No. 22-1267 took notice that "in the patent context, th[e] court has explained that a plaintiff need not "plead facts establishing that each element of an asserted claim is met," *In re Bill of Lading Transmission and Processing Sys. Pat. Litig.,* 681 F.3d 1323, 1335 (Fed. Cir. 2012) (citing *McZeal v. Sprint Nextel Corp.,* 501 F.3d 1354, 1357 (Fed. Cir. 2007)), but must plead "'enough fact[s] to raise a reasonable expectation that discovery will reveal' that the defendant is liable for the misconduct alleged." *Id.* at 1341 (alteration in original) (quoting *Twombly,* 550 U.S. at 556)".

The Federal Circuit in *Larry Golden v. Google LLC*; Case No. 22-1267 examined and determined Golden has described how the Google "smartphone", that include the ATAK software and CBRN plugin sensors literally infringes at least claim 5 of Golden's '287 Patent; claim 23 of Golden's '439 Patent; and claim 1 of Golden's '189 Patent. See the chart below:

Literal Infringement (Precedence)	**Literal Infringement (Fed. Cir. *Golden v. Google*)**
Literal infringement means that each and every element recited in a claim has identical correspondence in the allegedly infringing device or process. To literally infringe a patent, the accused system, method, etc. must include each limitation of a claim. E.g., *Southwall* (Fed. Cir. 05/10/95) To establish literal infringement, every limitation set forth in a claim must be found in an accused product, exactly. *Becton Dickinson* (Fed. Cir. 12/13/90). "Infringement, both literal and under the doctrine of equivalents, is an issue of fact."); *Cobalt Boats* (Fed. Cir. 05/31/19) "patent infringement is an issue of fact, tried by a jury" [U.S. CONST. amend. VII]	"Mr. Golden's complaint includes a detailed claim chart mapping features of an accused product, the [] Smartphone, to independent claims from U.S. Patent Nos. 10,163,287, 9,589,439, and 9,069,189 ... It [claim chart] attempts [] to map claim limitations to infringing product features, and it does so in a relatively straightforward manner ...[W]e conclude that the district court's decision in the Google case is not correct with respect to at least the three claims mapped out in the claim chart. Mr. Golden has made efforts to identify exactly how the accused products meet the limitations of his claims in this chart...."

The Federal Circuit in *Golden v. Google LLC* Case No. 22-1267 goes on to say: "In the Google case, the district court ***again*** concluded that Mr. Golden's complaint was frivolous. Here, however, Mr. Golden's complaint includes a detailed claim chart mapping features of an accused product, the Google [Pixel 5] Smartphone, to independent claims from U.S. Patent Nos. 10,163,287, 9,589,439, and 9,069,189" ... "to the extent that the chart includes the "exact same language" as previously rejected charts, it is simply the language of the independent claims being mapped to" ... "[i]t attempts—whether successfully or not—to map claim limitations to infringing product features, and it does so in a relatively straightforward manner. We conclude that the district court's decision in the Google case is not correct with respect to at least the three claims mapped out in the claim chart. Mr. Golden has made efforts to identify exactly how the accused products meet the limitations of his claims in this chart."

Although the Federal Circuit did not specifically say "without a doubt, Google's smartphone products that include the ATAK software and CBRN plugin sensors are literally and/or under the doctrine of equivalents, infringing Golden's patents asserted in the case", the Federal Circuit imply to say under the "clear and convincing evidence" standard, Google's smartphone products that include the ATAK software and CBRN plugin sensors are more likely than not is directly infringing Golden's patents asserted in the case. Therefore, Golden has satisfied his burden of proof under the "preponderance of evidence" standard with "enough fact[s] to raise a reasonable expectation that discovery will reveal' that the defendant is liable for the misconduct alleged." *Id.* at 1341 (alteration in original) (quoting *Twombly*, 550 U.S. at 556)".

In short, the co-conspirator Judge Rita F. Lin is precluded from re-litigating the issues already decided by the Federal Circuit. If Google believe the Circuit erred in their determination that Golden has pled "enough fact[s] to raise a reasonable expectation that discovery will reveal' that the defendant is liable for the misconduct alleged", Google should have filed a petition for review at the Supreme Court; if Google believes Golden's case is about the DoD DTRA ATAK CBRNE sensors, Google should have filed a petition for review at the Supreme Court; and, if Google disagrees with the Circuit and believes Golden's claim chart does not map features of an accused product, the Google Pixel 5 Smartphone, to independent claims from U.S. Patent Nos. 10,163,287, 9,589,439, and 9,069,189 ... and does so in a relatively straightforward manner, Google should have filed a petition for review at the Supreme Court.

The co-conspirator Judge Rita F. Lin gives more influence on the decisions from previous cases that victimized Golden in a judicial system of systemic and structural racism, judicial bias in favor of the white-owned corporation [Google], and, the deprivation of a Seventh Amendment right to a trial by jury, than to honor the decision handed down by a higher Federal Circuit court within the same jurisdiction.

CHAPTER TWO

PURSUANT TO 28 U.S.C. § 351(A): JUDGE RITA F. LIN HAS ENGAGED IN CONDUCT PREJUDICIAL TO THE EFFECTIVE AND EXPEDITIOUS ADMINISTRATION OF THE BUSINESS OF THE COURTS

Judge Rita F. Lin spent nineteen months--(09/14/2022 – 04/03/2024)—relitigating issues already decided by the Federal Circuit in *Larry Golden v. Google LLC,* Case No. 22-1267, and the United States Patent Trials and Appeals Board in the *Department of Homeland Security v. Larry Golden* Case No. IPR2014-00714.

Larry Golden v. Google LLC, Case No. 22-1267

Issue preclusion, also called collateral estoppel, means that a valid and final judgment binds Google and Judge Rita F. Lin as to same issues actually litigated and essential to the judgment in the first action.

In the first action the District Court of South Carolina dismissed Golden's complaint and claim charts as being "frivolous". On appeal in *Larry Golden v. Google LLC,* Case No. 22-1267 the Appellate Court "vacated and remanded" the case back to the District Court because the Federal Circuit found the complaint and the claim chart not to be facially frivolous. Therefore, it is the judgement of the superior Appellate Court that precludes Google, Northern District of California Court, Judge Rita F. Lin from relitigating certain issues already litigated.

The four essential elements to decide if issue preclusion applies are: 1) the former judgement must be valid and final; 2) the same issue is being brought; 3) the issue is essential to the judgement; 4) the issue was actually litigated.

Google and Judge Rita F. Lin are collateral estoppel from relitigating the same issues found in Golden's complaint and claim charts submitted in the South Carolina District Court case [*Golden v. Google*] that was found not to be facially frivolous by the Appellate Court in *Larry Golden v. Google LLC*; Case No. 22-1267.

Google and Judge Rita F. Lin are precluded from relitigating the pleading standards set forth in *Bell Atlantic Corp. v. Twombly,* 550 U.S. 544 (2007), and *Ashcroft v. Iqbal,* 556 U.S. 662 (2009) for this case that has already been decided by the Federal Circuit.

The Federal Circuit in *Golden v. Google LLC* Case No. 22-1267 disclosed in "Discussion" that the Circuit reviewed the case "under the pleading standards set forth in *Bell Atlantic Corp. v. Twombly,* 550 U.S.

544 (2007), and *Ashcroft v. Iqbal,* 556 U.S. 662 (2009), [a court must dismiss a complaint if it fails to allege "enough facts to state a claim to relief that is plausible on its face]." *Twombly,* 550 U.S. at 570; and, "plaintiff must allege facts that give rise to "more than a sheer possibility that a defendant has acted unlawfully." *Iqbal,* 556 U.S. at 678 (citation omitted)

> Three-Judge Panel: "DISCUSSION. 'Under the pleading standards set forth in *Bell Atlantic Corp. v. Twombly,* 550 U.S. 544 (2007), and *Ashcroft v. Iqbal,* 556 U.S. 662 (2009), a court must dismiss a complaint if it fails to allege "enough facts to state a claim to relief that is plausible on its face." *Twombly,* 550 U.S. at 570 … [T]his standard "requires more than labels and conclusions, and a formulaic recitation of the elements of a cause of action will not do." *Id.* at 555 (citation omitted). A plaintiff must allege facts that give rise to "more than a sheer possibility that a defendant has acted unlawfully." *Iqbal,* 556 U.S. at 678 (citation omitted) … this court has explained that a plaintiff … must plead "'enough fact[s] to raise a reasonable expectation that discovery will reveal' that the defendant is liable for the misconduct alleged."

The Federal Circuit in *Golden v. Google LLC* Case No. 22-1267 took notice that "in the patent context, th[e] court has explained that a plaintiff need not "plead facts establishing that each element of an asserted claim is met," *In re Bill of Lading Transmission and Processing Sys. Pat. Litig.,* 681 F.3d 1323, 1335 (Fed. Cir. 2012) (citing *McZeal v. Sprint Nextel Corp.,* 501 F.3d 1354, 1357 (Fed. Cir. 2007)), but must plead "'enough fact[s] to raise a reasonable expectation that discovery will reveal' that the defendant is liable for the misconduct alleged." *Id.* at 1341 (alteration in original) (quoting *Twombly*, 550 U.S. at 556)".

Judge Rita F. Lin and Google are precluded from relitigating the independent claims from U.S. Patent Nos. 10,163,287, 9,589,439, and 9,069,189". The Federal Circuit in *Larry Golden v. Google LLC*; Case No. 22-1267 examined and determined Golden has described how the Google "smartphone", that include the ATAK software and CBRN plugin sensors literally, and/or under the doctrine of equivalents, more likely than not, infringes at least claim 5 of Golden's '287 Patent; claim 23 of Golden's '439 Patent; and claim 1 of Golden's '189 Patent. See chart below:

Literal Infringement (Precedence)	**Literal Infringement (Fed. Cir. *Golden v. Google*)**
Literal infringement means that each and every element recited in a claim has identical correspondence in the allegedly infringing device or process. To literally infringe a patent, the accused system, method, etc. must include each limitation of a claim. E.g., *Southwall* (Fed. Cir. 05/10/95) To establish literal infringement, every limitation set forth in a claim must be found in an accused product, exactly. *Becton Dickinson* (Fed. Cir. 12/13/90). "Infringement, both	"Mr. Golden's complaint includes a detailed claim chart mapping features of an accused product, the Google Pixel 5 Smartphone, to independent claims from U.S. Patent Nos. 10,163,287, 9,589,439, and 9,069,189 ... It [claim chart] attempts [] to map claim limitations to infringing product features, and it does so in a relatively straightforward manner ...[W]e conclude that the district court's decision in the Google case is not correct with respect to at least the three claims mapped out in the claim chart. Mr. Golden has made efforts to identify

literal and under the doctrine of equivalents, is an issue of fact."); *Cobalt Boats* (Fed. Cir. 05/31/19) "patent infringement is an issue of fact, tried by a jury" [U.S. CONST. amend. VII]	exactly how the accused products meet the limitations of his claims in this chart…."

The Federal Circuit in *Golden v. Google LLC* Case No. 22-1267 goes on to say: "In the Google case, the district court again concluded that Mr. Golden's complaint was frivolous. Here, however, Mr. Golden's complaint includes a detailed claim chart mapping features of an accused product, the Google [Pixel 5] Smartphone, to independent claims from U.S. Patent Nos. 10,163,287, 9,589,439, and 9,069,189" … "to the extent that the chart includes the "exact same language" as previously rejected charts, it is simply the language of the independent claims being mapped to" … "[i]t attempts—whether successfully or not—to map claim limitations to infringing product features, and it does so in a relatively straightforward manner. We conclude that the district court's decision in the Google case is not correct with respect to at least the three claims mapped out in the claim chart. Mr. Golden has made efforts to identify exactly how the accused products meet the limitations of his claims in this chart."

Although the Federal Circuit did not specifically say "without a doubt, Google's smartphone products that include the ATAK software and CBRN plugin sensors are literally and/or under the doctrine of equivalents, infringing Golden's patents asserted in the case", the Federal Circuit imply to say under the "clear and convincing evidence" standard,

Google's smartphone products that include the ATAK software and CBRN plugin sensors are more likely than not is directly infringing Golden's patents asserted in the case.

> "Mr. Golden's complaint includes a detailed claim chart mapping features of an accused product, the Google Pixel 5 Smartphone, to independent claims from U.S. Patent Nos. 10,163,287, 9,589,439, and 9,069,189 ... It [claim chart] attempts [] to map claim limitations to infringing product features, and it does so in a relatively straightforward manner ...[W]e conclude that the district court's decision in the Google case is not correct with respect to at least the three claims mapped out in the claim chart. Mr. Golden has made efforts to identify exactly how the accused products meet the limitations of his claims in this chart...."

United States Department of Homeland Security v. Larry Golden Case IPR2014-00714

Judge Rita F. Lin and Google are also precluded from relitigating the construction for the patent claims' limitations for where and how the CBRNE device(s) can be found "within" the Google alleged infringing devices. In the *United States Department of Homeland Security v. Larry Golden* "Final Written Decision" Case IPR2014-00714, Entered: October 1, 2015, the PTAB construed "built in, embedded" as "something is included within, incorporated into, disposed within, affixed to, connected to, or mounted to another device, such that it is an integral part of the device".

In the Decision to Institute, we construed certain claim terms. Those constructions are reproduced in the chart below.

Claim Term	Construction
"built in, embedded" (claim 74)	"something is included within, incorporated into, disposed within, affixed to, connected to, or mounted to another device, such that it is an integral part of the device"
"communication device" (claim 81)	"monitoring equipment"

Dec. to Inst. 11–16.

No party challenges these constructions. Both of these terms were modified or removed in the amendment. To the extent that any of these constructions remain relevant after the amendment, we see no reason to modify them.

We further determined that no explicit construction was necessary for any other claim terms. Dec. to Inst. 10–11. Based on the record adduced during trial, we see no need to construe any other terms.

The Judge Rita F. Lin again erred in allowing Google to re-litigate issues that had already been adjudicated and a final decision was issued. The PTAB clearly stated the DTRA ATAK app and Draper's CBRNE Plug-in sensors are "an integral part of the device [Google smartphone]".

The federal circuit maintains that claim construction is not the type of legal question that should be resolved [or re-litigated] by a judge on the pleadings without the due consideration given in the *Markman* process.

The question presented is whether Judge Rita F. Lin and Google correctly held, consistent with the Supreme Court's instruction in *Markman v. Westview Instruments, Inc.* 517 U.S. 370, 372 (1996), that it is the province of the jury to determine whether an accused product infringes the claims of an asserted patent.

A *Markman* hearing is a court hearing in which a Judge determines the meaning of disputed words and phrases in a patent infringement lawsuit. A *Markman* hearing is also known as a construction hearing. When a Judge Rita F. Lin determines the meaning of the disputed words, it's called claim construction. But Judge Rita F. Lin is collateral estoppel from construing claim terms, or re-defining claim terms, already construed and a final decision was issued.

To determine patent infringement, a jury [not just Judge Rita F. Lin alone, with the Defense] must fully understand the definition of words used in the patent. A patented invention must be described with precise wording on its patent application. This wording and the defined definitions from the *Markman* hearing is what jurists use to determine if patent infringement has occurred.

In *Nalco v. Chem-Mod* (Fed. Cir. 2018), *Nalco* explained in detail its theory of infringement. For its part, the district court appeared to have conducted an informal claim construction that led to its ruling of no possible infringement.

Likewise, in the current case, the basic problem is Golden's patent claims do not include; nor expressly claim, the defendant's added limitation of "modified by a third-party in order to function", in the asserted patent claims limitations.

However, the Federal Circuit in *Nalco* rejected the lower court's informal claim construction as premature at the pleading stage:

> *"As Nalco explained, these disputes between the parties' hinge on [] what limitations are appropriate ... 'It is not appropriate to resolve these disputes, or to determine whether the method claimed in the '692 patent should be confined to the preferred embodiment, on a Rule 12(b)(6) motion, without the benefit of claim construction.' The purpose of a motion to dismiss is to test the sufficiency of the complaint, not to decide the merits."*

What does this mean within the confines of the current case – although claim construction is an issue of law, the Federal Circuit maintains that claim construction is not the type of legal question that should be resolved by a judge on the pleadings without the due consideration given in the *Markman* process. The Federal Circuit admonishes that invalidating any patent prior to claim construction is the exception rather than the rule. *Bancorp Servs., L.L.C. v. Sun Life Assurance Co. of Canada*, 687 F.3d 1266, 1274-75 ("[I]t will ordinarily be desirable—and often necessary—to resolve claim construction disputes prior to a § 101 analysis…").

Therefore, Judge Rita F. Lin erred in dismissing Golden's case on a limitation, function, action, or step that does not appear in any of Golden's patent claims asserted in this case, and is only fabricated by the defense.

Judge Rita F. Lin inappropriately dismissed Golden's case at the pleadings stage, with knowledge that Defendant's added "modified by a third-party in order to function" limitation does not appear in any of Golden's patent claims asserted in this case.

Golden believes Judge Rita F. Lin, needlessly spent over nineteen months re-litigating the term "modified". It doesn't matter that any of the devices, apparatuses, etc. capable of CBRNE detection were modified in order to function or not. What matters is, whether the devices, apparatuses, etc. capable of CBRNE detection was made an *integral part of the [smartphone] device* by means of being "built-in, embedded", "included within", "incorporated into", "disposed within", "affixed to", "connected to", or, "mounted to another device". Following is an example using two of the patent claims asserted in the current case:

> **Independent Claim 23 of Patent #: 9,589,439;** "A cell phone comprising: … 'whereupon the cell phone is ***interconnected*** to the cell phone detection device to receive signals or send signals to lock or unlock doors, to activate or deactivate security systems, to activate or deactivate multi-sensor detection systems, or to activate or deactivate the cell phone

detection device' ... 'the cell phone is at least a fixed, portable or mobile communication device ***interconnected*** to the cell phone detection device, capable of wired or wireless communication therebetween;'"

Independent Claim 1 of Patent #: 9,096,189; "A communication device of at least one of a cell phone, a smart phone, a desktop, a handheld, a PDA, a laptop, or a computer terminal ... 'the communication device is at least a fixed, portable or mobile communication device ***interconnected*** to a fixed, portable or mobile product, capable of wired or wireless communication therebetween' ... 'whereupon the communication device, is ***interconnected*** to a product equipped to receive signals from or send signals to lock or unlock doors, activate or deactivate security systems, activate or deactivate multi-sensor detection systems, or to activate or deactivate cell phone detection systems'"

Judge Rita F. Lin's overstep, is evidence the Judge has engaged in conduct prejudicial to the effective and expeditious administration of the business of the Court. In *Markman v. Westview Instruments, Inc.*, the Supreme Court held that patent infringement cases "must be tried to a jury," whose role is to "answer [] the ultimate question of infringement." 517 U.S. 370, 377, 385 (1996) (citing *Bischoff v. Whethered*, 76 U.S. 812, 814 (1869).

Judge Rita F. Lin has demonstrated she is not one skilled in the art to recognize the numerous alterations, modifications, and variations of

Golden's patented communicating, monitoring, detecting, and controlling (CMDC) invention. Judge Rita F. Lin is completely unaware of the structure and the novel way Golden created his patented CMDC devices. The Judge has made an unsuccessful attempt at hiding her ignorance of patent law, but cannot hide her prejudice and bias in favor of Google.

The Claims of a Patent Define the Invention

Judge Rita F. Lin is not allowed to add, convert, change, or modify the patent claim terms beyond the scope of the invention. "Modify by a third-party for the device to function" is no where to be found in the patent claims asserted in the case.

> "It is a bedrock principle of patent law," says the Federal Circuit Court of Appeals, that "the claims of a patent define the invention." *Innova/Pure Water, Inc. v. Safari Water Filtration Sys., Inc., 381 F.3d 1111, 1115 (Fed. Cir. 2004).* And the U.S. Supreme Court agrees: "the claims made in the patent are the sole measure of the grant." *Aro Mfg. Co. v. Convertible Top Replacement Co.*, 365 U.S. 336, 339 (1961). In the words of Judge Giles Rich, an author of the U.S. Patent Act of 1952, "the name of the game is the claim." Giles S. Rich, *The Extent of the Protection and Interpretation of Claims—American Perspectives*, 21 Int'l Rev. Indus. Prop. & Copyright L. 497, 499 (1990).

As noted above, Golden is reliant on the various types of "interconnection" to establish the functionality of his claimed inventions.

Interconnection is integral to achieving a globally connected digital ecosystem, allowing for seamless collaboration, innovation, and service delivery across continents. Interconnect, on the other hand, encompasses the establishment of multiple network connections, allowing various networks to interact and share data.

This can include connections between different types of networks, such as public and private, or between two networks with different service providers. Interconnect is more about creating a network ecosystem, facilitating a wide range of data exchanges, and offering flexibility and scalability in network architecture. https://www.flexential.com/resources/blog/ interconnection-examples

It is infeasible, or impractical for Golden to "modify" the smartphone device for every component, device, or apparatus that is located remote the smartphone device itself, such as GPS satellites, Cellular Towers, Smartwatches, Connected Vehicles, Internet-of-Things (IoTs) devices and sensors, and Remote Detection Devices. Modification is done on a per/event or per/ occurrence basis, whereby, if it's interconnected it's more alone the lines of being permanent.

The chart below illustrates the relevant patent claims' *elements* of Golden's asserted patents and how they are interconnected to various components remote the Google phone.

CLAIM CONSTRUCTION BASICS FOR INTERCONNECTING COMPONENTS AND IDENTIFYING ELEMENTS INSIDE THE ALLEGED INFRINGING SMARTPHONES		
Components	**Elements**	**Functions Substantially the Same as a *"Transceiver"***
Located ***remote*** the smartphones but are interconnected to the elements identified in the smartphones	Located ***inside*** the smartphones but are interconnected to the components identified remote the smartphones	The smartphone transceiver performs substantially the same function; in substantially the same way; to achieve substantially the same results
GPS Satellites	GPS Receiver	Receives radio waves from each satellite. Transmits the GPS data received, to track.
Cellular Towers	Primary Cellular Antenna	Receives and sends radio frequency (RF) signals
Smartwatch / Car	Bluetooth Antenna	Send and receive radio waves
Internet-of-Things (IoTs) [Devices and Sensors]	Cellular Modem	Translate data sent to and from the smartphone devices
Remote Detection Device	Operating System	Send and receive signals to enable communication between the devices' hardware and software

CHAPTER THREE

GOLDEN ALLEGES JUDGE RITA F. LIN KNOWINGLY VIOLATED GOLDEN'S CIVIL RIGHTS UNDER 42 U.S.C. § 1983 AND UNDER 18 U.S.C. § 242

The requirement of willfulness for a Judge Rita F. Lin to be prosecuted under section 2 of 18 U.S.C. § 242, which was enacted in the Civil Rights Act of 1866, is as follows: ("[C]itizens, of every race and color, without regard to any previous condition of slavery or involuntary servitude, . . . shall have the same right, in every State and Territory in the United States, . . . to full and equal benefit of all laws and proceedings for the security of person and property, as is enjoyed by white citizens, and shall be subject to like punishment, pains, and penalties, and to none other, any law, statute, ordinance, regulation, or custom, to the contrary notwithstanding.") *Civil Rights Act of 1866*, Ch. 31, § 1, 14 Stat. 27, 27

Congress requirement of willfulness for a judge to be prosecuted under section 2; responding to the critique that errors of judgment would lead to [Judge Rita F. Lin] being fined or imprisoned, Congress states: "[T]his is by no means [section 2's] purpose or its legal effect. The universal rule of law is that there can be no crime unless there be willful wrong. . .. [I]f an officer [Judge Rita F. Lin] shall intentionally deprive a citizen [Golden] of a right, knowing him to be entitled to it, then [the Judge] is guilty of a willful wrong which deserves punishment."

After numerous conversations and remarks about judges being open to prosecution due to section 2, in April of 1866, the Senate and the House of Representatives overrode President Johnson's veto, passing the Civil Rights Act of 1866 into law. *See Senate Vote #94 in 1866 (39th Congress.* In the years since its passage, section 2 has been revised and amended and now appears in the U.S. Code as 18 U.S.C. § 242, though it largely retains the original text of section 2 of the Civil Rights Act of 1866. *See 18 U.S.C. § 242*

Under 18 U.S.C. § 242, it is a crime for a person acting under color of law to willfully deprive a person [Judge Rita F. Lin] of a right or privilege protected by the Constitution or the laws of the United States. *See 18 U.S.C. § 242.* Consistent with the legislative history of the Civil Rights Act of 1866, the Supreme Court has held that ***judges are not immune*** from 18 U.S.C. § 242, stating:

> "[W]e have never held that the performance of the duties of judicial, legislative, or executive officers, requires or contemplates the immunization of otherwise criminal

> deprivations of constitutional rights. On the contrary, the judicially fashioned doctrine of official immunity does not reach "so far as to immunize criminal conduct proscribed by an Act of Congress . . .."

To highlight the point: despite criminal prosecutions inevitably having an effect on judicial behavior, and despite the fact that judicial immunity from criminal and civil suit was well established since the days of *Floyd v. Barker,* the Supreme Court has held that judges lack immunity from prosecution for violating constitutional rights under 18 U.S.C. § 242 because Congress acted to proscribe criminal conduct by judges in the Civil Rights Act of 1866.

This conclusion makes sense: after all, absolute judicial immunity was not universal in 1866, so the framers of what became 18 U.S.C. § 242 would not have needed to insert a clear statement in the text of the statute; it was obvious that the statute would open judges up to prosecution. Indeed, in the immediate aftermath of the Civil War, the prosecution of state judges for violating people's civil rights under a congressional statute was affirmed by the Supreme Court as a valid exercise of Congress's power. *See, e.g., Ex parte Virginia,* 100 U.S. 339, 348 (1880) (permitting criminal prosecution of state judge where state judge excluded Black jurors from jury selection in violation of the Constitution).

And in any event, if there were any doubt remaining, the Supreme Court enshrined the lack of judicial immunity from criminal prosecution under 18 U.S.C. § 242 in *O'Shea v. Littleton,* 414 U.S. 488, 503 (1974). *Imbler v. Pachtman,* 424 U.S. 409, 429 (1976), and *Dennis v. Sparks.* 449

U.S. 24, 31 (1980); see also *United States v. Lanier*, 520 U.S. 259, 269 (1997).

Finally, the Supreme Court failed to consider the legislative history of 42 U.S.C. § 1983, including its basis in 18 U.S.C. § 242. As the sponsor of the Ku Klux Klan Act of 1871 made clear, the text of 42 U.S.C. § 1983 was explicitly modeled on the text of 18 U.S.C. § 242. Moreover, this provision for civil liability was intended to be even more expansive than 18 U.S.C. § 242, even omitting in 42 U.S.C. § 1983 the requirement in 18 U.S.C. § 242 that violations be willful.

Just as members of Congress assumed that 18 U.S.C. § 242 would expose judges to criminal liability, a hypothesis that was later affirmed by the Supreme Court, members of Congress debating the Ku Klux Klan Act of 1871 also assumed that 42 U.S.C. § 1983 would expose judges to civil liability:

> "Every person who, under color of any statute, ordinance, regulation, custom, or usage, of any State or Territory or the District of Columbia, subjects, or causes to be subjected, any citizen of the United States or other person within the jurisdiction thereof to the deprivation of any rights, privileges, or immunities secured by the Constitution and laws, shall be liable to the party injured in an action at law, suit in equity, or other proper proceeding for redress, except that in any action brought against a judicial officer for an act or omission taken in such officer's judicial capacity, injunctive relief shall not be granted unless a declaratory decree was violated or declaratory

relief was unavailable." *42 U.S. Code § 1983 - Civil action for deprivation of rights*

Golden alleges Judge Rita F. Lin, with knowledge, willfully violated Golden's Seventh Amendment constitutional right to a trial by jury.

Example of How Judge Rita F. Lin Knowingly and Willingly Violated Golden's Civil Rights by allowing the White-owned Google company the opportunity to Re-structure the Company's dealings before determining liability for Google's current offenses.

Judicial Conduct and Disability Act

28 U.S.C. § 351(a): "Any person alleging that a judge has engaged in conduct prejudicial to the effective and expeditious administration of the business of the courts" may file a written complaint.

Willful Misconduct

Judge Rita F. Lin's "willful misconduct" refers to the Judge knowingly requiring Golden to prove direct infringement under 28 U.S.C. § 1498(a) as a necessary predicate to proving direct infringement under 35 U.S.C. § 271(a). *Zoltek III*

In this current case, *Larry Golden v. Google LLC*, NDC Case 3:22-cv-05246-RFL AMENDED COMPLAINT against Google LLC, Dkt. 42; Filed 08/23/23. Golden informed the Court that an amended complaint was necessary because "Google has discontinued the making, offering for sell, and selling of the Google Pixel 5 Smartphone; discontinued the use of Qualcomm's Snapdragon chipset, thereby eliminating Golden's "joint infringement" claim; and discontinued offering for sell, and selling, the ATAK-Military on Google Play, to avoid liability for the actions brought against them"

> "This amended complaint is necessary because after the Federal Circuit's order on 09/08/2022, in *Larry Golden v. Google LLC*; Case No. 22-1267, to "VACATE AND REMAND" the relevant Case No: 22-1267 Document 15; back to the District Court "to be filed and request service of process", Google has discontinued the making, offering for sell, and selling of the Google Pixel 5 Smartphone; discontinued the use of Qualcomm's Snapdragon chipset, thereby eliminating Plaintiff's "joint infringement" claim; and discontinued offering for sell, and selling, the ATAK-Military on Google Play, to avoid liability for the actions brought against them."

Upon information and belief, the presiding Judge ordered the amended complaint because he believed Golden claims of patent infringement was no longer valid because of the actions of Google to stop selling the Google Pixel 5; stop using Qualcomm's alleged infringing CPU/chipset; and stop selling the ATAK-Military software app in the Google Play store. All three components were significant to the decision made in *Larry Golden v. Google LLC*; Case No. 22-1267, to "VACATE AND REMAND" the case. Back to the District Court.

The "Reversed Engineered" Claim Chart Presented to the Federal Circuit is proof Judge Rita F. Lin Knowingly violated Golden's Civil Rights by Re-litigating Issues already decided, while depriving Golden of his Seventh Amendment right to a Trial by Jury

This is not an argument of the merits of the case. Golden is simply pointing out that Judge Rita F. Lin herself verified the Federal Circuits findings. Judge Rita F. Lin determined there could be no infringement unless the Google phone is modified by a third-party to function.

Golden agrees with Judge Rita F. Lin because it's what Golden have been pleading throughout this entire case. Judge Lin identified certain claim limitations (see the chart below) that requires modification to function, in accordance with Golden's claim limitations.

Judge Rita F. Lin identified Draper's CBRNE Plug-in seniors and the DTRA ATAK software; she recites from Golden's claim limitations, qualifies for direct infringement under the doctrine of equivalents because the CBRNE Plug-in seniors and the DTRA ATAK software combination performs substantially the same function; in substantially the same way; to achieve the same result! *Jenkinson Co. v. Hilton Davis Chem. Co. (1997)*

The following Claim Chart is a duplicate of the Claim Chart submitted on appeal to the Federal Circuit in *Larry Golden v. Google LLC*; Case No. 22-1267. The chart illustrates show the "reverse engineering" Google's alleged literal infringement and/or infringement under the doctrine of equivalents of Golden's '287, '439, and '189 patents.

Google Pixel 5 Smartphone	Patent #: 10,163,287; Independent Claim 5	Patent #: 9,589,439; Indep. Claim 23	Patent #: 9,096,189; Independent Claim 1
	A monitoring device, comprising:	A cell phone comprising:	A communication device of at least one of a cell phone, a smart phone, a desktop, a handheld, a PDA, a laptop, or a computer terminal …
CPU: Octa-core (1 × 2.4 GHz Kryo 475 Prime & 1 × 2.2 GHz Kryo 475 Gold & 6 × 1.8 GHz Kryo 475 Silver) System-on-a-chip: Qualcomm Snapdragon 765G	at least one central processing unit (CPU);	a central processing unit (CPU) for executing and carrying out the instructions of a computer program;	at least one of a central processing unit (CPU) for executing and carrying out the instructions of a computer program, …
Ambient Temperature sensor supported by the Android platform. Measures the ambient room temperature in degrees Celsius (°C). Monitoring air temperatures.	at least one temperature sensor in communication with the at least one CPU for monitoring temperature;	X	X

Gravity sensor supported by the Android platform. Measures the force of gravity in m/s2 that is applied to a device on all three physical axes (x, y, z). Motion detection (shake, tilt, etc.).	at least one motion sensor in communication with the at least one CPU;	X	X
Light sensor supported by the Android platform. Measures the ambient light level (illumination) in lx. Controlling screen brightness. Screen: 6-inch flexible OLED display at 432 ppi	at least one viewing screen for monitoring in communication with the at least one CPU;	X	X
Connectivity: Wi-Fi 5 (a/b/g/n/ac) 2.4 + 5.0 GHz, Bluetooth 5.0 + LE, NFC, GPS (GLONASS, Galileo, BeiDou), eSIM capable	at least one global positioning system (GPS) connection in communication with the at least one CPU;	at least one of a satellite connection, Bluetooth connection, WiFi connection, internet connection, radio frequency (RF) connection, cellular connection, ... or GPS connection;	at least one satellite connection, Bluetooth connection, WiFi connection, internet connection, radio frequency (RF) connection, cellular connection, ... short-range radio frequency (RF) connection, or GPS connection;

Connectivity: Wi-Fi 5 (a/b/g/n/ac) 2.4 + 5.0 GHz, Bluetooth 5.0 + LE, NFC, GPS (GLONASS, Galileo, BeiDou), eSIM capable	at least one of an internet connection or a Wi-Fi connection in communication with the at least one CPU;	wherein at least one of... WiFi connection, internet connection, radio frequency (RF) connection, cellular connection... capable of signal communication with the transmitter or the receiver;	wherein the only type or types of communication with the transmitter and the receiver of the communication device and transceivers of the products is a type or types selected from the group... of satellite, Bluetooth, WiFi...
Connectivity: Wi-Fi 5 (a/b/g/n/ac) 2.4 + 5.0 GHz, Bluetooth 5.0 + LE, NFC, GPS (GLONASS, Galileo, BeiDou), eSIM capable	at least one of a Bluetooth connection, a cellular connection, or a satellite connection in communication with the at least one CPU;	at least one of a... Bluetooth connection, WiFi connection, internet connection... cellular connection... short range radio frequency (RF) connection, or GPS connection;	X

Google's Android operating system features a lock mechanism ... known as pattern lock. To set, drag your finger along [] the screen. To unlock, replicate the pattern drawn. ... the phone locks and cannot be unlocked without logging int... Google Nest × Yale Lock ... you can lock or unlock door from your phone.	at least one locking mechanism in communication with the at least one CPU for locking the communication device, the at least one locking mechanism configured to at least one of engage (lock) the ... device, disengage (unlock) the ... device, or disable (make unavailable) the ... device;	whereupon the cell phone is interconnected to the cell phone detection device to receive signals or send signals to lock or unlock doors, to activate or deactivate security systems, to activate or deactivate multi-sensor detection systems, or to activate or deactivate the cell phone detection device;	X
Pixel phones use USB-C with USB 2.0 power adapters and cables. To charge your phone with a USB-A power adapter, use a USB-C to USB-A cable.	at least one power source comprising at least one of a battery, electrical connection, or wireless connection, to provide power to the communication device;	X	X

BIOMETRICS: Biometric factors allow for secure authentication on the Android platform. The Android framework includes face and fingerprint biometric authentication. Android can be customized to support other forms of biometric authentication (such as Iris).	at least one biometric sensor in communication with the at least one CPU for providing biometric authentication to access the communication device;	wherein the cell phone is equipped with a biometric lock disabler that incorporates at least one of a fingerprint recognition, voice recognition, face recognition, ... such that the cell phone is locked by the biometric lock disabler to prevent unauthorized use; and	wherein the communication device is equipped with a biometric lock disabler ... of a fingerprint recognition, ... face recognition... of the cell phone, the smart phone, the desktop, ... the laptop or the computer terminal is locked by the biometric lock disabler to prevent unauthorized use
Android Team Awareness Kit, ATAK (built on the Android operating system) ... a single interface for ... different CBRN-sensing technologies... a wearable smartwatch that measures ..., heart rate) or a device mounted on a drone to detect chemical warfare agents.	at least one sensor for chemical, biological, or human detection in communication with the at least one CPU;	the cell phone is at least a fixed, portable or mobile communication device interconnected to the cell phone detection device, capable of wired or wireless communication therebetween; and	the communication device is at least a fixed, portable or mobile communication device interconnected to a fixed, portable or mobile product, capable of wired or wireless communication therebetween...

Android Team Awareness Kit, ATAK (built on the Android operating system) is a digital application available to warfighters throughout the DoD. ATAK— on an end-user device such as a smartphone or a tablet. With DTRA's contribution, ATAK now includes ... (CBRN) plug-ins.	one or more detectors in communication with the at least one CPU for detecting at least one of chemical, biological, radiological, or explosive agents;	at least one of a chemical sensor, a biological sensor, an explosive sensor, a human sensor, a contraband sensor, or a radiological sensor capable of being disposed within, on, upon or adjacent the cell phone;	wherein the communication device receives a signal via any of one or more products listed in any of the plurality of product grouping categories;
Connectivity: Wi-Fi 5 (a/b/g/n/ac) 2.4 + 5.0 GHz, Bluetooth 5.0 + LE, NFC, GPS (GLONASS, Galileo, BeiDou), eSIM capable	at least one radio-frequency near-field communication (NFC) connection in communication with the at least one CPU...	X	X

Google Nest × Yale Lock is connected to the Nest app; you can lock or unlock your door from your phone. *Android Team Awareness Kit,* ATAK (built on the Android operating system) provides a single interface for viewing and controlling different CBRN-sensing tech.	at least one of a transmitter or a transceiver in communication with … CPU configured to send signals to … detect at least one of a chemical biological… agent … device is capable of communicating, monitoring, detecting, and controlling.	a transmitter for transmitting signals and messages to a cell phone detection device; a receiver for receiving signals from the cell phone detection device;	a transmitter for transmitting signals and messages to at least one of plurality product groups …, a cell phone detection device… locking device; a receiver for receiving signals, data or messages from at least one of … a cell phone detection device… locking device;
Google Nest × Yale Lock is connected to the Nest app; you can lock or unlock your door from your phone. *Android Team Awareness Kit,* ATAK (built on the Android operating system) provides a single interface for viewing and controlling different CBRN-sensing tech.	X	X	whereupon the communication device, is interconnected to a product equipped to receive signals from or send signals to lock or unlock doors, activate or deactivate security systems, activate or deactivate multi-sensor detection systems, or to activate or deactivate cell phone detection systems

Android Team Awareness Kit, ATAK ATAK offers warfighters geospatial mapping for situational awareness during combat — on an end-user device such as a smartphone or a tablet. With DTRA's contribution, ATAK now … (CBRN) plug-ins.	X	a transmitter for transmitting signals and messages to a cell phone detection device; a receiver for receiving signals from the cell phone detection device;	wherein at least one …, Bluetooth connection, WiFi connection, internet connection, … cellular connection, … signal communication with the transmitter and the receiver of the …device and transceivers of the products;
Android Team Awareness Kit, ATAK ATAK offers warfighters geospatial mapping for situational awareness during combat — on an end-user device such as a smartphone or a tablet. With DTRA's contribution, ATAK now includes CBRN) plug-ins.	X	whereupon a signal sent to the receiver of the cell phone detection device from … chemical sensor, the biological sensor, the explosive sensor, … or the radiological sensor, causes a signal that includes at least one of location data …	X

The United States has both statutory equivalents doctrine that is codified in 35 U.S.C. § 112, which extends to equivalents available at patent's issuance, "[t]he specification shall contain a written description of the invention, and of the manner and process of making and using it, in such full, clear, concise, and exact terms as to enable any person skilled in the art to which it pertains, or with which it is most nearly connected, to make and use the same, and shall set forth the best mode contemplated by the inventor or joint inventor of carrying out the invention", and "[t]he specification shall conclude with one or more claims particularly pointing out and distinctly claiming the subject matter which the inventor or a joint inventor regards as the invention." (*35 U.S. Code § 112 – Specification (a)(b)*), and a more general (non-statutory, created by courts) doctrine of equivalents, which extends to technological equivalents developed after the patent is granted. *Warner-Jenkinson Co. v. Hilton Davis Chem. Co. (1997)*

> "In American practice, the doctrine of equivalents analysis is applied to individual claim limitations, not to the invention as a whole. The legal test, articulated in *Warner-Jenkinson Co. v. Hilton Davis Chem. Co. (1997)*, is whether the difference between the feature in the accused device and the limitation literally recited in the patent claim is 'insubstantial'."

"One way of determining whether a difference is 'insubstantial' or not is called the 'triple identity' test. Under the triple-identity test, the difference between the feature in the accused device and the limitation literally recited in the patent claim may be found to be "insubstantial" if the feature in the accused device:

1. Performs substantially the same function
2. In substantially the same way

3. To obtain the same result

as the limitation literally recited in the patent claim. See *Graver Tank & Manufacturing Co. v. Linde Air Products Co., (1950).*

CHAPTER FOUR

THE JUDGE FAIL TO STRICTLY FOLLOW THE DECISION(S) HANDED DOWN BY THE HIGHER COURT WITHIN THE SAME JURISDICTION

Judge Rita F. Lin is in violation of the doctrine of *vertical stare decisis* for not honoring the decision of the higher Appellate Court in *Larry Golden v. Google LLC*; Case No. 22-1267:

> The Northern District of California Court Judge, who is bound by and must follow the decisions of the U.S. Court of Appeals for the Federal Circuit [*vertical stare decisis*] fail to abide by the Circuit's decision in *Larry Golden v. Google LLC* Case No. 22-1267, that Google's "smartphone" literally and/or under the doctrine of equivalents infringes Golden's "independent claims from U.S. Patent Nos. 10,163,287, 9,589,439, and 9,069,189 ...

and it does so in a relatively straightforward manner". The District Court Judge was bound by the doctrine of *vertical stare decisis*, to uphold the CAFC's decision.

Vertical stare decisis binds lower courts to follow strictly the decisions of higher courts within the same jurisdiction (e.g., the Northern District of California Court Judge must follow the decisions of the U.S. Court of Appeals for the Federal Circuit). The Supreme Court defines *vertical stare decisis* as the doctrine, "a lower court must strictly follow the decision(s) handed down by a higher court within the same jurisdiction".

Judge Rita F. Lin engages in *vertical stare decisis* when she applies precedent from the higher court. For example, if the Northern District of California Court Judge in *Golden v. Golden* adhered to a previous ruling from the United States Court of Appeals for the Federal Circuit, in *Larry Golden v. Google LLC*; Case No. 22-1267, that would be *vertical stare decisis.*

The bigger question is why? Why did Judge Rita F. Lin ignore the ruling from the higher court and decided to be the defendant; the judge; and the jury? "But for" the Judge is racially bias against Golden and is more concern with earning the respect of her co-conspirators who supports a judicial system of systemic and structural racism.

Standard Claim Charts – I

The claim chart presented and reviewed by the Federal Circuit in *Larry Golden v. Google LLC*; Case No. 22-1267 is based on "reverse engineering". Reverse engineering, also called "tear down", is a method or process to discover how the DTRA ATAK software and/or its Draper CBRNE Plug-in Sensors functions with a Google smartphone product.

In Golden's patent specifications: "[p]roduct grouping 2 (sensors) include, but are not limited to, chemical, biological, [] motion sensors, [] biometric sensors, [] human..." Golden, during patent prosecution was able to get the "heart-rate sensor" allowed as the species of the sensors listed above, to include the signature sensor (i.e., unique cardiac signature) as genesis.

Therefore, one way to read the following standard claim chart is to read it from the Google smartphone; to the Google smartwatch; to the Google smartwatch chemical, biological, motion, biometric, human, or signature "heart-rate" sensor. Another way to read the standard claim chart is to identify exactly where the element can be found (CPU, transmitter, receiver, transceiver, GPS receiver, and the antennas for Bluetooth, cellular and Wi-Fi).

Although Golden is not required to plead infringement on an element-by-element basis at the pleading stage, Golden not only plead infringement on an element-by-element basis at the Federal Circuit in *Larry Golden v. Google LLC*; Case No. 22-1267 with a reverse engineered claim chart, Golden also pled infringement on an element-by-element basis that can be read two ways with the standard claim chart in this current case *Golden v. Google LLC*; NDC Case 3:22-cv-05246-RFL. Why would Judge Rita F. Lin not consider Golden's evidence?

The following standard claim chart was presented to Judge Lin for an element-by-element analysis of a Google smartphone and how it functions with a Google smartwatch CBRNE sensing for claim 1 of '189 patent; claim 23 of '439 patent; and claim 5 of '287 patent.

	Google Smartwatch CBR Detector for Smartphone
 ATAK (built on the Google Android operating system) … controlling different CBRN-sensing technologies, whether that is a wearable smartwatch that measures a warfighter's vitals (e.g., heart rate) …	The US Military's Latest Wearables [Smart Watch] Can Detect Illness Two Days Before You Get Sick https://www.defenseone.com/technology/2020/09/military s-latest-wearables-can-detect-illness-two-days-you-get-sick/168664/ Studies reveal smartwatch biometrics can detect COVID-19: "smartwatches and other wearables measuring biometrics like heart-rate variability have the ability to detect if a person is COVID-19 positive" https://www.biometricupdate.com/202101/studies-reveal-smartwatch-biometrics-can-detect-covid-19-before-symptoms-surface Homeland Security's Smartwatch Will Detect Nuclear Bombs https://www.popular-mechanics.com/military/research/a18161/homeland-security -smartwatch-detect-nuclear-bombs/

IDENTIFYING IN THE ALLEGED INFRINGING SMARTPHONE WHERE EACH ELEMENT IS FOUND THAT LITERALLY AND/OR UNDER THE DOCTRINE OF EQUIVALENTS INFRINGES GOLDEN'S PATENTS.	
Google Pixel 8 Smartphone	Patent No. 9,096,189 (claim 1 of the '189 patent)
Golden has identified the Google smartphone(s) as "a communication device" and the Google Pixel smartwatch as the multi-sensor detection device or a cell phone detection device	***A communication device*** of at least one of a cell phone, a smart phone, a desktop, a handheld, a PDA, a laptop, or a computer terminal for monitoring products, interconnected to a product for communication therebetween, comprising:
Golden has identified the Google "Tensor" as the CPU/Chipset for executing and carrying out instructions for the Google Pixel smartphone; the Qualcomm SW5100 / Cortex M33 co-processor CPU/Chipset for executing and carrying out instructions for the Google Pixel smartwatch	at least one of a central processing unit (CPU) for executing and carrying out the instructions of a computer program ... or a front-end processor for communication between a host computer and other devices;
The Google Pixel smartphone transceiver connects the Smartwatch (i.e., multi-sensor detection device, or cell phone detection device) to the Google Pixel smartphone via Bluetooth	a transmitter for transmitting signals and messages to at least one of plurality product groups based on the categories of a multi-sensor detection device ... a cell phone detection
The Google Pixel smartphone transceiver connects the Smartwatch (i.e., multi-sensor detection device, or	a receiver for receiving signals, data or messages from at least one of plurality product groups based on the categories of a multi-

cell phone detection device) to the Google Pixel smartphone via Bluetooth	sensor detection device ... a cell phone detection device
Golden has identified the Google smartphone(s) as "a communication device" and the Google Pixel smartwatch as the multi-sensor detection device or a cell phone detection device for wireless communication therebetween	the communication device is at least a ... mobile communication device interconnected to a fixed, portable or mobile product, capable of wired or wireless communication therebetween;
The Google Pixel smartphone transceiver connects the Smartwatch (i.e., multi-sensor detection device, or cell phone detection device) to the Google Pixel smartphone via Bluetooth	at least one satellite connection, Bluetooth connection, WiFi connection, internet connection, radio frequency (RF) connection, cellular connection, broadband connection, long and short-range radio frequency (RF) connection, or GPS connection;
The Google Pixel smartphone transceiver connects the Smartwatch (i.e., multi-sensor detection device, or cell phone detection device) to the Google Pixel smartphone via Bluetooth	wherein at least one satellite connection, Bluetooth connection, WiFi connection, internet connection, radio frequency (RF) connection, cellular connection, broadband connection, long and short-range radio frequency (RF) connection is capable of signal communication with the transmitter and the receiver of the communication device and transceivers of the products;

Golden has identified the Google smartphone(s) fingerprint or facial recognition and the Google Pixel smartwatch as having voice recognition. "*Google Assistant voice commands on Google Pixel Watch*" https://support.google.com/googlepixelwatch/answer/12677020?hl=en	wherein the communication device is equipped with a biometric lock disabler that incorporates at least one of a fingerprint recognition, voice recognition, face recognition, hand geometry, retina scan, iris scan and signature such that the communication device that is at least one of the cell phone, the smart phone, the desktop, the handheld, the PDA, the laptop or the computer terminal is locked by the biometric lock disabler to prevent unauthorized use;

IDENTIFYING IN THE ALLEGED INFRINGING SMARTPHONE WHERE EACH ELEMENT IS FOUND THAT LITERALLY AND/OR UNDER THE DOCTRINE OF EQUIVALENTS INFRINGES GOLDEN'S PATENTS.	
Google Pixel 8 Smartphone	**Patent No. 9,589,439 (claim 23 of the '439 patent)**
Golden has identified the Google smartphone(s) as "a new, improved upon, and useful cell phone" and the Google Pixel smartwatch as the multi-sensor detection device or a cell phone detection device	***A cell phone comprising:***

Golden has identified the Google "Tensor" as the CPU/Chipset for executing and carrying out instructions for the Google Pixel smartphone; the Qualcomm SW5100 / Cortex M33 co-processor CPU/Chipset for executing and carrying out instructions for the Google Pixel smartwatch	a central processing unit (CPU) for executing and carrying out the instructions of a computer program;
The Google Pixel smartphone transceiver connects the Smartwatch (i.e., multi-sensor detection device, or cell phone detection device) to the Google Pixel smartphone via Bluetooth	a transmitter for transmitting signals and messages to a cell phone detection device;
The Google Pixel smartphone transceiver connects the Smartwatch (i.e., multi-sensor detection device, or cell phone detection device) to the Google Pixel smartphone via Bluetooth	a receiver for receiving signals from the cell phone detection device;
Golden has identified the Google smartphone(s) as "a communication device" and the Google Pixel smartwatch as the multi-sensor detection device or a cell phone detection device for wireless communication therebetween, and	the cell phone is at least a fixed, portable or mobile communication device interconnected to the cell phone detection device, capable of wired or wireless communication therebetween;

Golden is identifying the Google Pixel smartphone(s) as "a new, improved upon, and useful cell phone" or "communication device", interconnected to the Google Pixel smartwatch as the cell phone detection device to receive signals or send signals to activate or deactivate	whereupon the cell phone is interconnected to the cell phone detection device to receive signals or send signals to ... activate or deactivate multi-sensor detection systems, or to activate or deactivate the cell phone detection device;
Golden is identifying the Google Pixel smartwatch as the multi-sensor detection device or a cell phone detection device for CBRNE detection, that is adjacent the Google Pixel smartphone(s) as "a new, improved upon, and useful cell phone" or "communication device"	at least one of a chemical sensor, a biological sensor, an explosive sensor, a human sensor, a contraband sensor, or a radiological sensor capable of being disposed within, on, upon or adjacent the cell phone
The Google Pixel smartphone transceiver connects the Smartwatch (i.e., multi-sensor detection device, or cell phone detection device) to the Google Pixel smartphone via Bluetooth	at least one of a satellite connection, Bluetooth connection, WiFi connection, internet connection, radio frequency (RF) connection, cellular connection, broadband connection, long range radio frequency (RF) connection, short range radio frequency (RF) connection, or GPS connection;

The Google Pixel smartphone transceiver connects the Smartwatch (i.e., multi-sensor detection device, or cell phone detection device) to the Google Pixel smartphone via Bluetooth	wherein at least one of the satellite connection, Bluetooth connection, WiFi connection, internet connection, radio frequency (RF) connection, cellular connection, broadband connection, long range radio frequency (RF) connection, short range radio frequency (RF) connection, or GPS connection is capable of signal communication with the transmitter or the receiver;
Golden has identified the Google smartphone(s) fingerprint or facial recognition and the Google Pixel smartwatch as having voice recognition. "*Google Assistant voice commands on Google Pixel Watch*" https://support.google.com/googlepixelwatch/answer/12677020?hl=en	wherein the cell phone is equipped with a biometric lock disabler that incorporates at least one of a fingerprint recognition, voice recognition, face recognition, hand geometry, retina scan, iris scan, or signature such that the cell phone is locked by the biometric lock disabler to prevent unauthorized use;

IDENTIFYING IN THE ALLEGED INFRINGING SMARTPHONE WHERE EACH ELEMENT IS FOUND THAT LITERALLY AND/OR UNDER THE DOCTRINE OF EQUIVALENTS INFRINGES GOLDEN'S PATENTS.	
Google Pixel 8 Smartphone	**Patent No. 10,163,287 (claim 5 of the '287 patent)**
Golden has identified the Google smartphone(s) as "a monitoring device" and the Google Pixel smartwatch as the multi-sensor detection device or a cell phone detection device	***A monitoring device, comprising:***
Golden has identified the Google "Tensor" as the CPU/Chipset for executing and carrying out instructions for the Google Pixel smartphone; the Qualcomm SW5100 / Cortex M33 co-processor CPU/Chipset for executing and carrying out instructions for the Google Pixel smartwatch	at least one central processing unit (CPU);
Golden has identified the Wi-Fi 7 (802.11be) with 2.4GHz+5GHz+6GHz,2x2+ 2x2 MIMO of the Google Pixel smartphone that is in communication with the Google "Tensor" CPU/Chipset]; and the Wi-Fi 802.11 b/g/n 2.4GHz that is in communication with the Google	at least one of an internet connection or a Wi-Fi connection in communication with the at least one CPU;

Pixel smartwatch; the Qualcomm SW5100 / Cortex M33 co-processor CPU/Chipset	
Golden has identified the Bluetooth® v5.3 with dual antennas for enhanced quality of the Google Pixel smartphone that is in communication with the Google "Tensor" CPU/Chipset]; and the Bluetooth® 5.0 that is in communication with the Google Pixel smartwatch; the Qualcomm SW5100 / Cortex M33 CPU/Chipset	at least one of a Bluetooth connection, a cellular connection, or a satellite connection in communication with the at least one CPU;
Golden has identified the Google Pixel smartphone as an NFC-enabled device that communicates in one or both directions uses a frequency of 13.56 MHz in the globally available unlicensed radio frequency ISM band that is in communication with the Google "Tensor" CPU/Chipset; and the NFC connectivity of the Google Pixel Smartwatch that is in communication with the Qualcomm SW5100 / Cortex M33 co-processor CPU/Chipset	at least one radio-frequency near-field communication (NFC) connection in communication with the at least one CPU;

The Google Pixel smartphone is equipped with the ability to check a "human" heart rate i.e. the number of beats per minute with the smartphone camera, and the working camera flash unit that is in communication with the Google "Tensor" CPU/Chipset; and check a "human" heart rate with the multi-path optical heart rate sensor of the Google Pixel smartwatch that is in communication with the Qualcomm SW5100 / Cortex M33 co-processor CPU/Chipset	at least one sensor for chemical, biological, or human detection in communication with the at least one CPU;
Golden is identifying the Google Pixel smartwatch as the multi-sensor detection device or a cell phone detection device for CBRNE detection, that is in communication with the Google Pixel smartphone "Tensor" CPU/Chipset; and in communication with the Google Pixel smartwatch Qualcomm SW5100 / Cortex M33 co-processor CPU/Chipset	one or more detectors in communication with the at least one CPU for detecting at least one of chemical, biological, radiological, or explosive agents;

Golden is identifying the Google Pixel smartphone(s), that is in communication with the Google "Tensor" CPU/Chipset, as "a new, improved upon, and useful cell phone" or "communication device", interconnected to the Google Pixel smartwatch, that is in communication with the Qualcomm SW5100 / Cortex M33 co-processor CPU/Chipset, as the cell phone detection device capable of receiving signals or sending signals	at least one of a transmitter or a transceiver in communication with the at least one CPU configured to send signals to monitor ... or send signals to detect at least one of a chemical biological, radiological, or explosive agent such that the communication device is capable of communicating, monitoring, detecting, and controlling.

Standard Claim Charts – II

In Golden's patent specifications: "[p]roduct grouping 2 (sensors) include, but are not limited to, chemical, biological, [] motion sensors, [] biometric sensors, [] human..." Golden, during patent prosecution was able to get the "heart-rate sensor" allowed as the species of the sensors listed above, to include the signature sensor (i.e., unique cardiac signature) as genesis.

Therefore, one way to satisfy the asserted patent claims requirement for detection of at least the sensors listed in the above paragraph is with the Google smartphone camera "heart-rate" sensor (i.e., chemical, biological, motion, biometric, human, or signature "heart-rate" sensor).

The Google Fit app., that is preinstalled on the Google Pixel handset, is used to measure a heart rate on the Google Pixel phone. Google Pixel smartphones are capable of monitoring a heart rate even though there isn't any dedicated hardware in the handset to track these metrics. It instead uses a smart approach that leverages the phone's rear camera.

Within the Google Fit app, the user will be able to track their heart rate and their respiratory rate. The user will need a compatible smartphone to be able to do this though, which includes every Google Pixel handset since the Google Pixel 3 and Google Pixel 3 XL.

Another way is to identify exactly where each element can be found in the alleged infringing Google smartphone device, that include identifying where the CPU, transmitter, receiver, transceiver, GPS receiver, and the antennas for Bluetooth, cellular and Wi-Fi can be located that are at least interconnected to the components, devices, or apparatuses capable of CBRNE detection.

Although Golden is not required to plead infringement on an element-by-element basis at the pleading stage, Golden not only plead infringement on an element-by-element basis at the Federal Circuit in *Larry Golden v. Google LLC*; Case No. 22-1267 with a reverse engineered claim chart, Golden also pled infringement on an element-by-element basis that can be read two ways with the standard claim chart in this current case *Golden v. Google LLC*; NDC Case 3:22-cv-05246-RFL. Why would Judge Rita F. Lin not consider Golden's evidence?

Lastly, the following claim chart of patent claims that was reviewed by the Federal Circuit in *Golden v. Google*; Case No. 22-1267, and presented to Judge Rita F. Lin for an element-by-element analysis between claim 1 of'189 patent; claim 23 of'439 patent; and claim 5 of'287 patent, and the alleged infringing Google smartphone product, is illustrated below. The Google smartphone camera designed for CBR detection is ***internal*** the Google smartphone.

Camera [1 2] Used for Detecting Chem/Bio Agents.

1 The camera captures the image from the array of nanopores that uses fluid rather than bulky moving parts. The sensors contained in one array is determined by the resolution phone camera. The resolution in cell phone cameras; probe a million different spots on the sensor simultaneously. *Tiny sensors tucked into cell phones could map airborne toxins in real time.* Source: https:// www.understanding nano.com/cell-phone-sensors-toxins.html

2 Hyperspectral imaging scans for light frequencies that humans can't see in order to identify the unique chemical signatures of different substances. They say their device, which can be mass

produced, is compatible with all standard smartphone cameras. *These New Smartphone Cameras Could Tell You What an Object Is Made of* https://www.sciencealert.com/new-smartphone-cameras-could-tell-you-what-an-object-is-made-of

The Google "megapixel" Camera is "Native" to the Manufacture of the Google Pixel Smartphone	
Patent No. 9,096,189 (Patent Claim 1 of Golden's '189 Patent)	**Google "megapixel Camera; embedded in the Google Pixel Smartphone, and interconnected for communication, therebetween**
A communication device of at least one of a cell phone, a smart phone, a desktop, a handheld, a PDA, a laptop, or a computer terminal for monitoring products, interconnected to a product for communication therebetween, comprising:	[Golden has identified the Google smartphone(s) as "a communication device" and the Google "megapixel" Camera as the multi-sensor detection device or a cell phone detection device]
at least one of a central processing unit (CPU) for executing and carrying out the instructions of a computer program ... or a front-end processor for communication between a host computer and other devices;	[Golden has identified the Google "Tensor" as the CPU/Chipset for executing and carrying out instructions for the Google Pixel smartphone; the Google "Tensor" CPU/Chipset for executing and carrying out instructions for the Google "megapixel" Camera]

a transmitter for transmitting signals and messages to at least one of plurality product groups based on the categories of a multi-sensor detection device ... a cell phone detection device ...;	[The Google Pixel smartphone transceiver connects the Google "megapixel" Camera (i.e., multi-sensor detection device, or cell phone detection device) to the Google Pixel smartphone via Bluetooth]
a receiver for receiving signals, data or messages from at least one of plurality product groups based on the categories of a multi-sensor detection device ... a cell phone detection device ...;	[The Google Pixel smartphone transceiver connects the Google "megapixel" Camera (i.e., multi-sensor detection device, or cell phone detection device) to the Google Pixel smartphone via Bluetooth]
the communication device is at least a ... mobile communication device interconnected to a fixed, portable or mobile product, capable of wired or wireless communication therebetween;	[Golden has identified the Google smartphone(s) as "a communication device" and the Google "megapixel" Camera as the multi-sensor detection device or a cell phone detection device for wireless communication therebetween]
at least one satellite connection, Bluetooth connection, WiFi connection, internet connection, radio frequency (RF) connection, cellular connection, broadband connection, long and short-range radio frequency (RF) connection, or GPS connection;	[The Google Pixel smartphone transceiver connects the Google "megapixel" Camera (i.e., multi-sensor detection device, or cell phone detection device) to the Google Pixel smartphone via Bluetooth]

wherein at least one satellite connection, Bluetooth connection, WiFi connection, internet connection, radio frequency (RF) connection, cellular connection, broadband connection, long and short-range radio frequency (RF) connection is capable of signal communication with the transmitter and the receiver of the communication device and transceivers of the products;	[The Google Pixel smartphone transceiver connects the Google "megapixel" Camera (i.e., multi-sensor detection device, or cell phone detection device) to the Google Pixel smartphone via Bluetooth]

The Google "megapixel" Camera is "Native" to the Manufacture of the Google Pixel Smartphone	
Patent No. 9,589,439 (Patent Claim 23 of Golden's '439 patent)	Google "megapixel Camera; embedded in the Google Pixel Smartphone, and interconnected for communication, therebetween
A cell phone comprising	[Golden has identified the Google smartphone(s) as "a new, useful, and improved upon cell phone" and the Google "megapixel" Camera as the multi-sensor detection device or a cell phone detection device]

a central processing unit (CPU) for executing and carrying out the instructions of a computer program;	[Golden has identified the Google "Tensor" as the CPU/Chipset for executing and carrying out instructions for the Google Pixel smartphone; the Google "Tensor" CPU/Chipset for executing and carrying out instructions for the Google "megapixel" Camera]
a transmitter for transmitting signals and messages to a cell phone detection device;	[The Google Pixel smartphone transceiver connects the Google "megapixel" Camera (i.e., multi-sensor detection device, or cell phone detection device) to the Google Pixel smartphone via Bluetooth]
a receiver for receiving signals from the cell phone detection device;	[The Google Pixel smartphone transceiver connects the Google "megapixel" Camera (i.e., multi-sensor detection device, or cell phone detection device) to the Google Pixel smartphone via Bluetooth]
the cell phone is at least a fixed, portable or mobile communication device interconnected to the cell phone detection device, capable of wired or wireless communication therebetween;	[Golden has identified the Google smartphone(s) as "a new, useful, and improved upon cell phone" and the Google "megapixel" Camera as the multi-sensor detection device or a cell phone detection device for wireless communication therebetween],

at least one of a chemical sensor, a biological sensor, an explosive sensor, a human sensor, a contraband sensor, or a radiological sensor capable of being disposed within, on, upon or adjacent the cell phone	[Golden is identifying the Google "megapixel" Camera as the multi-sensor detection device or a cell phone detection device for CBRNE detection, that is embedded in the Google Pixel smartphone(s) as "a new, improved upon, and useful cell phone" or "communication device"]
at least one of a satellite connection, Bluetooth connection, WiFi connection, internet connection, radio frequency (RF) connection, cellular connection, broadband connection, long range radio frequency (RF) connection, short range radio frequency (RF) connection, or GPS connection;	[The Google Pixel smartphone transceiver connects the Google "megapixel" Camera (i.e., multi-sensor detection device, or cell phone detection device) to the Google Pixel smartphone via Bluetooth]
wherein at least one of the satellite connection, Bluetooth connection, WiFi connection, internet connection, radio frequency (RF) connection, cellular connection, broadband connection, long range radio frequency (RF) connection, short range radio frequency (RF) connection, or GPS connection is capable of signal communication with the transmitter or the receiver;	[The Google Pixel smartphone transceiver connects the Google "megapixel" Camera (i.e., multi-sensor detection device, or cell phone detection device) to the Google Pixel smartphone via Bluetooth]

wherein the cell phone is equipped with a biometric lock disabler that incorporates at least one of a fingerprint recognition, voice recognition, face recognition, hand geometry, retina scan, iris scan, or signature such that the cell phone is locked by the biometric lock disabler to prevent unauthorized use;	[Golden has identified the Google smartphone(s) fingerprint recognition and the Google "megapixel" Camera as having facial recognition.

The Google "megapixel" Camera is "Native" to the Manufacture of the Google Pixel Smartphone	
Patent No. 10,163,287 (Patent Claim 5 of Golden's '287 patent)	**Google "megapixel Camera; embedded in the Google Pixel Smartphone, and interconnected for communication, therebetween**
A monitoring device, comprising:	[Golden has identified the Google smartphone(s) as "a monitoring device" and the Google "megapixel" Camera as the multi-sensor detection device or a cell phone detection device]
at least one central processing unit (CPU);	[Golden has identified the Google "Tensor" as the CPU/Chipset for executing and carrying out instructions for the Google Pixel smartphone; the Google "Tensor" CPU/Chipset for executing and

	carrying out instructions for the Google "megapixel" Camera]
at least one of an internet connection or a Wi-Fi connection in communication with the at least one CPU;	[Golden has identified the Wi-Fi 7 (802.11be) with 2.4GHz+5GHz+6GHz,2x2+ 2x2 MIMO of the Google Pixel smartphone and the Google "megapixel" Camera that is in communication with the Google "Tensor" CPU/Chipset]
at least one of a Bluetooth connection, a cellular connection, or a satellite connection in communication with the at least one CPU;	[Golden has identified the Bluetooth® v5.3 with dual antennas for enhanced quality of the Google Pixel smartphone and the Google "megapixel" Camera that is in communication with the Google "Tensor" CPU/Chipset]
at least one radio-frequency near-field communication (NFC) connection in communication with the at least one CPU;	[Golden has identified the Google Pixel smartphone as an NFC-enabled device that communicates in one or both directions uses a frequency of 13.56 MHz in the globally available unlicensed radio frequency ISM band that is in communication with the Google "Tensor" CPU/Chipset]

at least one sensor for chemical, biological, or human detection in communication with the at least one CPU;	The Google Pixel smartphone is equipped with the ability to check a "human" heart rate i.e. the number of beats per minute with the smartphone camera, and the working camera flash unit that is in communication with the Google "Tensor" CPU/Chipset]
one or more detectors in communication with the at least one CPU for detecting at least one of chemical, biological, radiological, or explosive agents	[Golden is identifying the Google "megapixel" Camera as the multi-sensor detection device or a cell phone detection device for CBRNE detection, that is in communication with the Google Pixel smartphone "Tensor" CPU/Chipset]
at least one of a transmitter or a transceiver in communication with the at least one CPU configured to send signals to monitor ... or send signals to detect at least one of a chemical biological, radiological, or explosive agent such that the communication device is capable of communicating, monitoring, detecting, and controlling.	[Golden is identifying the Google Pixel smartphone(s), that is in communication with the Google "Tensor" CPU/Chipset, as "a monitoring device" or "communication device", interconnected to the Google "megapixel" Camera as the cell phone detection device capable of receiving signals or sending signals]

CHAPTER FIVE

CONTRIBUTORY INFRINGEMENT: JUDGE RITA F. LIN VIOLATED GOLDEN'S "DUE PROCESS" RIGHT WHEN SHE FRUSTRATED THE FAIRNESS OF THE PROCEEDINGS

Although the Fifth Amendment "Due Process" Clause is brief, important parts of the Supreme Court's constitutional doctrine rest on it. At the most general level, the clause reiterates the principle of the rule of law: the government [Judge Rita F. Lin] must act in accordance with legal rules and not contrary to them.

A more specific application of the Clause is the doctrine today called "procedural due process," which concerns the fairness and lawfulness of decision-making methods used by the courts [Judge Rita F. Lin] and the executive.

Governmental actors [Judge Rita F. Lin] violate due process when [she] frustrates the fairness of proceedings. Likewise, fair notice and the opportunity to be heard are due process requirements in criminal, civil, and other proceedings.

Judge Rita F. Lin Acknowledges Google knew Golden's Patents are Infringed by the Combination:

At the very least, in order to reach liability for contributory infringement, Google must know of Golden's patents to be liable for its contributory infringement: "§ 271(c) requires knowledge of the existence of the patent that is infringed." *Global-Tech* (U.S. 05/31/2011) (calling this "§ 271(c)'s intent requirement."). But the statute implies more: "knowing the same to be especially made or especially adapted for use in an infringement of such patent," suggesting that accused party must know there is an infringement.

The Supreme Court has held that the statute requires knowledge of infringement: "On this question a majority of the Court is of the view that § 271(c) does require a showing that the alleged contributory infringer Google knew that the ***combination*** for which his component was especially designed was both patented and infringing." *Aro Mfg.* (Aro II) (U.S. 06/08/1964); "In *Aro II,* a majority held that a violator of § 271(c) must know 'that the ***combination*** for which his component was especially designed was both patented and infringing,' 377 U.S., at 488,

Both Google and the co-conspirator Judge Rita F. Lin knew the CBRNE devices allegedly infringes Golden's patents when combined with the Google smartphones:

"Plaintiff's complaint alleges that ATAK is not made by Google, and he does not allege that ATAK comes pre-loaded on Google phones: Through collaboration and innovation, the Defense Threat Reduction Agency has integrated its powerful, hazard-awareness-and-response tools into the Android Tactical Assault Kit (or the Android Team Awareness Kit, ATAK). ATAK is a digital application available to warfighters throughout the DoD. Built on the Android operating system, ATAK offers warfighters geospatial mapping for situational awareness during combat — on an end-user device such as a smartphone or a tablet. With DTRA's contribution, ATAK now includes chemical, biological, radiological, and nuclear (CBRN) plug-ins." *Golden v. Google* Case 3:22-cv-05246-RFL Document 41 Filed 08/10/23

"The FAC alleges five theories of direct infringement (id. ¶ 75, Exs. G & H), all of which suffer from the same defect for which the original complaint was dismissed: the theories all require that the accused products be modified in some way for them to infringe on the patents-in-suit. ... "Mr. Golden's allegations, even if true, at best establish that [defendant's] smartphones might be modified post-sale to perform the accused detector/sensor functionality, which is not enough for direct infringement on the claims here." *Golden v. Google* Case 3:22-cv-05246-RFL Document 68 Filed 04/03/24

ATAK application: "finding that the defendants' products "do not infringe without modification—the modification of installing the required software". [gateway to the alleged infringing Draper CBRNE Plug-in sensors]

***NFC tags*:** "Golden' second theory [] requires combining "Google's NFC sensor," which are allegedly embedded in the accused products, with external NFC tags that have been converted to detect certain chemicals in order for there to be alleged infringement."

***Camera sensors*:** "The FAC also alleges that "[s]martphones provide hardware and software capability which can be incorporated with [CBR] sensors, enabling accurate on-site portable sensing," further confirming that the sensors are separate devices that may be "incorporated" into the smartphone. (Id.) Therefore, this theory of infringement also fails because the accused products do not infringe without modification."

***Smartphone biosensors*:** "The diagram shows an "add on device" with the alleged biosensors (i.e., "capillary inlet," "microfluidic cassette," VIS-NIR spectrometer, and "NNAP electrodes") attached to a nondescript smartphone. (Id.) As such, this theory also requires modification to the accused smartphones to state an infringement claim."

***Google Beacon*:** Golden's fifth theory (see Ex. G at 34–41) fails for the same reason, as it requires "Google Beacon," which the FAC's own illustrations show is a separate device from the accused smartphones." *Golden v. Google* Case 3:22-cv-05246-RFL Document 68 Filed 04/03/24

Unlike the lie Judge Rita F. Lin implied, "[t]he FAC alleges five theories of direct infringement"; the FAC actually alleges five theories of indirect [contributory] infringement, whereby the Google smartphone is the "material part" of the alleged infringing CBRNE devices listed above and illustrated in the claim chart below:

CBRNE — Multi-Sensor Detection Systems	
Draper designed a chemical, biological, radiological and nuclear (CBRN) Plugin to enable users to integrate CBRN sensors into TAK, collect CBRN sensor data, display it on a map and livestream it across the TAK network to other users. CBRN plugins for ATAK, WinTAK and WebTAK are operational in the field. https://www.draper.com/explore-solutions/tak **ATAK-CIV (CBRN):** "The Tactical Assault Kit is DoD nomenclature for the Team Awareness Kit (TAK) application: a mission planning, geospatial, Full Motion Video (FMV), and system administrator tool that reduces the operational footprint from a tactical laptop, to a commercial mobile device.	

Data can be pre-loaded into ATAK or downloaded from the network when available." https://play.google.com/store/apps/details?id=com.atakmap.app.civ&hl=en_US&gl=US	
Near-Field Communication (NFC) Smartphone Sensor: Nascent technology embedded in modern smartphones—near-field communication (NFC)—for wireless electronic, portable, non-line-of-sight selective detection of gas-phase chemicals *(Fig. 1)* National Institutes of Health (NIH). *"Wireless gas detection with a smartphone via rf nfc communication"* Published online 2014 Dec 8. doi: 10.1073/pnas. 1415403111 Retrieved from: https://www.ncbi.nlm.nih.gov/pmc/articles/PMC4280584/	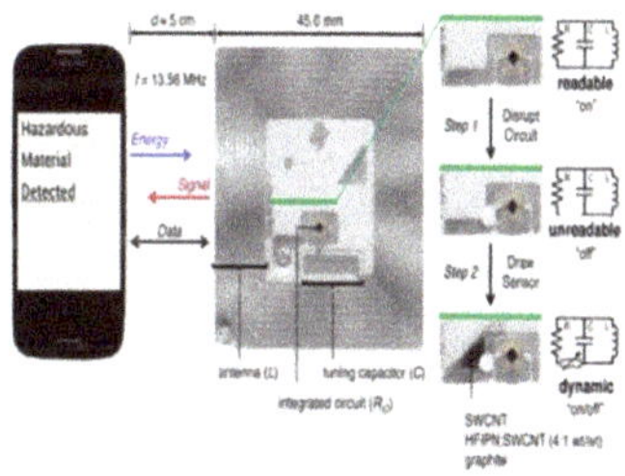 ***Figure 1*** Conversion of an NFC tag into a CARD enables wireless rf detection of chemical analytes with a smartphone. NFC-enabled smartphones communicate with NFC tags by simultaneously energizing the NFC tag with an alternating magnetic field (f = 13.56 MHz) through inductive coupling and transferring data by signal modulation.

Camera Sensor: Camera lens in cell phone with microfluidic lens functions as camera; uses microscope to focus on a chemical sensor. A ***megapixel*** camera captures the image from array of nanopores uses fluid rather than bulky moving parts. The sensors in one array is determined by the ***pixel*** resolution phone camera. ***Megapixel*** resolution in cell phone cameras; probe a million different spots simultaneously. *Tiny sensors tucked into cell phones could map airborne toxins in real time.* Source: https://www.understandingnano.com/cell-phone-sensors-toxins.html

Hyperspectral imaging scans for light frequencies that humans can't see in order to identify the unique chemical signatures of different substances. They say their device, which can be mass produced, is compatible with all standard smartphone cameras. *These New Smartphone Cameras Could Tell You What an Object Is Made of* https://www.sciencealert.com/new-smartphone-cameras-

Smartphones provide hardware and software capability which can be incorporated with [CBR] sensors, enabling accurate on-site portable sensing. The camera, screen, and LED flashlight of the smartphone can be employed as components of the sensor. https://link. springer.com/article/10.1007/s11468-022-01672-1

<table>
<tr>
<td>Smartphone Biosensors:
1. Ambient light sensor: Cancer biomarkers; Toxic metals; Pathogens
2. Capillary inlet: (Air analysis). Airborne Pathogens; Aerosols
3. Capillary inlet: (Fluid analysis). Blood analysis; Biomarkers
4. Microfluidic cassette: Interchangeable cassettes with varying assays
5. VIS-NIR spectrometer: Food freshness; Melanoma
6. NNAP Electrodes: Toxic metals and Organic pollutants in water
7. Optical Waveguide: Pathogens in water and food
8. Back and front camera: Image analysis; Colorimetric analysis
9. Microphone: Voice recording stress levels</td>
<td>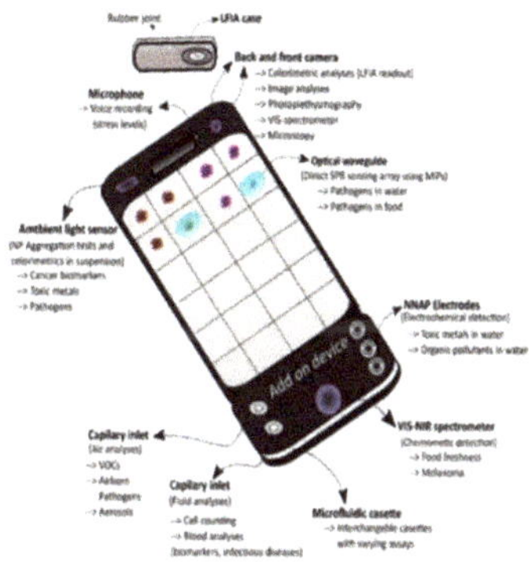
</td>
</tr>
<tr>
<td>Google Beacon: Bluetooth; GPS; Wi-Fi
Google Android smart phones and WiFi/Bluetooth beacons as detectors and sources. Google smart phone sensors (GPS, WiFi, Bluetooth) and beacon signals to calculate distance between detector and source. Filtering WiFi/ Bluetooth ranging functions and GPS</td>
<td></td>
</tr>
</table>

<table>
<tr>
<td>location data. Filtering GPS derived distances based on jump in calculated position or when GPS reports jump in position but phone accelerometer sensors do not show rapid acceleration. Specific models in different categories of radiation instruments (dosimeters, survey meters, personal radiation detectors, backpacks, nuclide identifiers, and mobile systems).</td>
<td>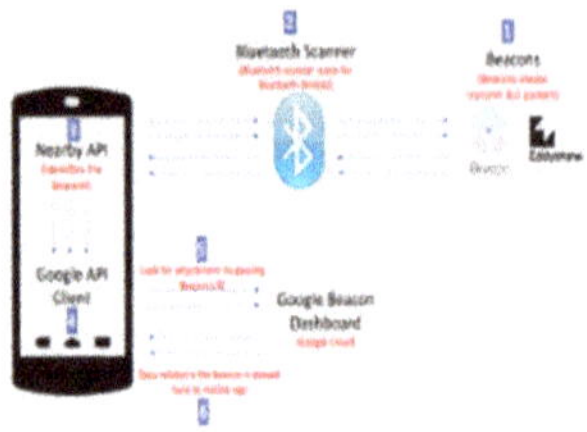

Google Beacon is a type of Bluetooth technology with proximity-based triggers. These triggers affect both the physical and digital world. Using Bluetooth low energy (BLE) hardware technology, beacons communicate with nearby smart devices like smartphones, tablets, etc. Different types of beacons that perform different tasks.</td>
</tr>
</table>

Multi-Sensor Detection System — CBRNE

Multi-Sensor Detection Systems	**Patent #: 9,589,439; Independent Claim 19**	**Patent #: 9,096,189; Independent Claim 7**
CBRNE Smartwatch, CBR Smartphone Camera,	A multi-sensor detection system for detecting at least one explosive, nuclear, contraband, chemical,	A multi-sensor detection system for detecting at least one explosive, nuclear, contraband, chemical,

CBR—NFC Smartphone Sensors CBR Smartphone Beacon (Bluetooth) Smartphone Biosensors CBRNE Plug-in Sensors	biological, human, radiological agent, or compound, comprising:	biological, human, or radiological agents and compounds, comprising:
CBRNE Smartwatch, CBR Smartphone Camera, CBR—NFC Smartphone Sensors CBR Smartphone Beacon (Bluetooth) Smartphone Biosensors CBRNE Plug-in Sensors	a plurality of sensors for detecting at least one chemical, biological, radiological, explosive, nuclear, human, or contraband agent or compound, capable of being disposed within, on, upon or adjacent a multi-sensor detection device;	a plurality of sensors for detecting at least one chemical, biological, radiological, explosive, nuclear, human or contraband agents and compounds and capable of being disposed within, on, upon or adjacent a multi sensor detection device;

Built on the Android, iOS, and Windows operating system for connecting the software (i.e., ATAK) and the hardware – CBRN sensors and detectors		
The Smartphones and Smartwatches of Google, Qualcomm, LG, Apple, and Samsung; and, the Laptops, Tablets, and Desktop PCs of Intel and Samsung	monitoring equipment comprising at least one of a computer, personal computer (PC), laptop, notebook PC, handheld, cell phone, personal digital assistant (PDA) or smart phone for at least one of a receipt or transmission of signals therebetween;	monitoring equipment comprising at least one of plurality product groups based on the categories of a computer, laptop, notebook, PC, handheld, cell phone, PDA or smart phone for the receipt and transmission of signals therebetween;
The Smartphone(s) [Google Pixel 8] connects to a cell tower or base station via radio waves, and that tower is usually physically connected to the infrastructure	at least one cell phone tower interconnected to the monitoring equipment for sending signals thereto and receiving signals therefrom or at least one satellite capable of	at least one cell phone tower interconnected to the monitoring equipment for sending signals thereto and receiving signals therefrom or at least one satellite capable of

to send that data wherever it needs to go. Satellite communication on smartphones. The iPhone 14 is the first smartphones widely available in the market that support satellite connectivity. Android 15 extends platform support for satellite connectivity. The platform now has UI elements that are needed to "ensure a consistent user experience across the satellite connectivity landscape."	transmitting signals to the monitoring equipment;	transmitting signals to the monitoring equipment;
The Smartphone(s) [Google Pixel 8] connects to a cell tower or base station via radio waves, and that tower is usually physically connected to the infrastructure to send that data	at least one satellite or at least one cell phone tower capable of signal communication between the multi-sensor detection device and the monitoring equipment;	at least one satellite or at least one cell phone tower capable of signal communication between the multi sensor detection device and the monitoring equipment;

wherever it needs to go. Satellite communication on smartphones. The iPhone 14 is the first smartphones widely available in the market that support satellite connectivity. Android 15 extends platform support for satellite connectivity. The platform now has UI elements that are needed to "ensure a consistent user experience across the satellite connectivity landscape."		
The internet connection is shared by many smartphone functions on the Google Pixel 8 smartphone such as internet browsing, receiving email messages and installing apps. Wi-Fi	at least one internet connection capable of communication between the multi-sensor detection device and the monitoring equipment;	at least one internet connection capable of communication between the multi sensor detection device and the monitoring equipment;

is a method for devices such as the Google Pixel 8 smartphone to connect wirelessly to the Internet using radio waves.		
Sit(x) is a commercial Server-as-a-Service solution based developed by PAR Government for the U.S. Defense & Intelligence Community. Sit(x) has real-time communication and information sharing. With Sit(x), individuals and teams can communicate via personal computers and handheld mobile [Google Pixel 8 smartphone] devices by voice or text. They can share real-time full-motion video (FMV), airborne/drone	whereupon a signal sent to a receiver of the multi-sensor detection device from a satellite; or to a cell phone tower; or through at least one of a short-range radio frequency or a long-range radio frequency; causes a signal to be sent to the monitoring equipment that includes at least one of location data or sensor data;	whereupon a signal sent to a receiver of the multi sensor detection device from a satellite; or to a cell phone tower; or through short and/or long-range radio frequency; causes a signal to be sent to the monitoring equipment that includes location data and sensor data;

imagery, GPS locations, photos, and satellite imagery.		
The '287, '439 & '189 patent specs: Product grouping (PG) 1 (storage & transportation); PG 2 (sensors); PG 3 (detector case; modified and adapted); PG 4 (monitoring & communication devices); PG 5 (communication methods); PG 6 (biometrics); and, PG 7 (authorized person)	wherein the monitoring equipment or multi-sensor detection device receives a signal via any of one or more products of any product grouping categories;	wherein the monitoring equipment or multi sensor detection device receives a signal via any of one or more products listed in any of the plurality of product grouping categories;
The Android-based [Google] smartphone[s] now contained integrated satellite … Wi-Fi is a method for Google Pixel 8 smartphone to connect wirelessly to	wherein at least one of a satellite connection, Bluetooth connection, WiFi connection, internet connection, radio frequency (RF) connection, cellular connection, broadband connection, long	wherein at least one satellite connection, Bluetooth connection, WiFi connection, internet connection, radio frequency (RF) connection, cellular connection, broadband connection, long and

the Internet using radio waves... The internet connection is shared by many functions on the Google Pixel 8 smartphone such as internet browsing, email messaging; installing apps... The Google Pixel 8 phone connects to a cell tower or base station via radio waves, and that tower is usually physically connected to the infrastructure to send that data...	range radio frequency connection, or short-range radio frequency (RF) connection is capable of signal communication with the transmitter, a receiver of the monitoring equipment, the multi-sensor detection device, or transceivers of the products;	short-range radio frequency (RF) connection is capable of signal communication with the transmitter and the receiver of the monitoring equipment or multi sensor detection device and transceivers of the products;
BIOMETRICS: Biometric factors allow secure authentication on the Google Android platform. The Google Android framework includes face and	wherein the monitoring equipment is equipped with a biometric lock disabler that incorporates at least one of a fingerprint recognition, voice	wherein the monitoring equipment is equipped with a biometric lock disabler that incorporates at least one of a fingerprint recognition, voice

fingerprint biometric authentication. The Smartphones and Smartwatches of Google, Qualcomm, LG, Apple, and Samsung; and, the Laptops, Tablets, and Desktop PCs of Intel and Samsung	recognition, face recognition, hand geometry, retina scan, iris scan or signature such that the monitoring device that is at least one of the computer, the laptop, the notebook, the PC, the handheld, the cell phone, the PDA, or the smart phone is locked by the biometric lock disabler to prevent unauthorized use;	recognition, face recognition, hand geometry, retina scan, iris scan and signature such that the monitoring device that is at least one of the computer, the laptop, the notebook, the PC, the handheld, the cell phone, the PDA, or the smart phone is locked by the biometric lock disabler to prevent unauthorized use;
The Android-based [Google] smartphone[s] now contained integrated satellite ... Wi-Fi is a method for devices such as the Google Pixel 8 smartphone to connect wirelessly to the Internet using radio waves...	wherein the only type or types of communication with the transmitter and the receiver of the communication device and transceivers of the products is a type or types selected from the group consisting of satellite, Bluetooth, WiFi, internet, radio frequency (RF),	wherein the only type or types of communication with the transmitter and the receiver of the communication device and transceivers of the products is a type or types selected from the group consisting of satellite, Bluetooth, WiFi, internet, radio frequency (RF),

The internet connection is shared by many ATAK functions on the Google Pixel 8 smartphone such as internet browsing, receiving email messages; installing apps... The Google Pixel 8 phone connects to a cell tower or base station via radio waves, and that tower is usually physically connected to the infrastructure to send that data wherever it needs to go.	cellular, broadband, long range radio frequency, and short-range radio frequency (RF).	cellular, broadband, and long and short-range radio frequency (RF).

"Whoever [Google LLC] offers to sell or sells within the United States [] a component [smartphone] of a [] combination [] or apparatus for use in practicing a patented process, constituting a material part of the invention, knowing the same to be especially made or especially adapted for use in an infringement of such patent, and not a staple article or commodity of commerce suitable for substantial noninfringing use, shall be liable as a contributory infringer." *35 U.S.C. § 271(c).*

As this is a "contributory" liability doctrine, there must be a direct infringement for there to be Sec. 271(c) liability. Golden alleged the multi-sensor detection systems of a CBRNE Smartwatch, a CBR Smartphone Camera, a CBR—NFC Smartphone Sensor, a CBR Smartphone Beacon, Smartphone Biosensors, and CBRNE Plug-in Sensors infringes Golden's patents.

CHAPTER SIX

WHEN JUDGE RITA F. LIN UNLAWFULLY SEPERATED GOLDEN'S PATENTED INVENTION COMBINATION, THE JUDGE ALSO KNOWINGLY CHANGED THE CAUSES OF ACTION FOR THE ALLEGED INFRINGING PRODUCTS

Initially, Golden alleged Google's Pixel 5 smartphone directly infringed Golden's patents; Golden alleged the Google Android Open-Source Operating System platform is the device (software) Google used to induced the infringement of Golden's patents; and Qualcomm contributed to the infringement of Golden's patents with its Snapdragon CPU/Chipset that has no substantial non-infringing use.

Golden also informed the Court that DTRA ATAK software and Draper's CBRNE Plug-in Sensors combination also allegedly infringes

Golden's patents, but a claim of direct infringement was not entered in this Court for or by Golden for lack of subject matter jurisdiction. A claim of direct infringement for the alleged patented combination should be made in the United States Court of Federal Claims.

Upon receiving notice that the Federal Circuit in *Larry Golden v. Google LLC*; Case No. 22-1267 "vacated and remanded" the case back to the District Court because the Federal Circuit determined that Google more likely than not, directly (literally) infringed Golden's patents, Google discontinued the making, using, offering for sell, and selling the of the Google Pixel 5 smartphones and selling the ATAK-MIL software from its Google Play store; and discontinued the contract with Qualcomm for its Snapdragon CPU/Chipset.

Judge Rita F. Lin immediately overstepped the jurisdiction of the Northern District of California and demanded Golden prove direct infringement of the ATAK software and Draper CBRNE Plug-in sensors under 28 U.S.C. § 1498(a) as a necessary predicate to proving direct infringement under 35 U.S.C. § 271(a). Which means proving the Government's ATAK infringe.

In complying with Judge Rita F. Lin's demand that Golden prove direct infringement of Golden's multi-sensor detection device(s) and/or Golden's cell phone detection device(s) of at least that of a CBRNE Smartwatch, a CBR Smartphone Camera, a CBR—NFC Smartphone Sensor, a CBR Smartphone Beacon, Smartphone Biosensors, and CBRNE Plug-in Sensors, Golden submitted to the Court a claim chart identifying the alleged infringement of Golden's patented inventions. *See the claim chart in the previous section of this document.*

The claim chart in the previous section of this document, also illustrates how the Google Pixel smartphone series contributes to the infringement of Golden's multi-sensor detection device(s) and/or Golden's cell phone detection device(s) of at least that of a CBRNE Smartwatch, a CBR Smartphone Camera, a CBR—NFC Smartphone Sensor, a CBR Smartphone Beacon, Smartphone Biosensors, and CBRNE Plug-in Sensors. Golden only needs to show that the distinct and separate "components" has no substantial non-infringing use.

> Labeling it "an important, and previously unresolved, question," a 2-1 panel held that contributory infringement arises where sold devices (optical disc drives) "contain hardware or software components that have no substantial non-infringing use [ ]," even though device has other hardware and embedded software module that cannot be used to infringe—distinguishing *Hodosh* (Fed. Cir. 11/25/87) and relying on *Grokster* (U.S. 06/27/2005) ("one who distributes a device with the object of promoting its use to infringe [ ], as shown by clear expression or other affirmative steps taken to foster infringement, is liable for the resulting acts of infringement by third parties.") *Ricoh* (Fed. Cir. 12/23/08).
>
> *In re Bill of Lading* (Fed. Cir. 06/07/12) ("Where the product is equally capable of, and interchangeably capable of both

infringing and substantial non-infringing uses, a claim for contributory infringement does not lie."; distinguishing *Ricoh*

The following claim chart was presented to the Judge Rita F, Lin for an element-by-element analysis of products Google's alleged infringing smartphone product and how it functions with the Google Tensor CPU / Chipset designed to carry out the operational and functional instructions of the Google smartphone. Which means the Google Smartphone series and the Google Tensor CPU/Chipset; both contributes to the infringement of Golden's patents.

Google Tensor; Tensor 2; and Tensor 3	**Patent #: 10,984,619; Independent Claim 1**	**Patent #: 10,984,619; Independent Claim 11**
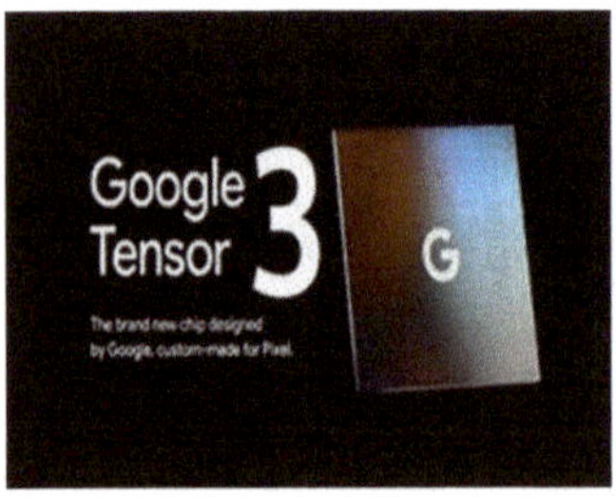 ***The Google Tensor (i.e. CPU; Chipset)*** is considered the "brain" of the Smartphone, …	***A communication device*** that is at least a personal computer (PC), a cellphone, a smartphone, a laptop, or a handheld scanner, comprising at least a central processing unit (CPU), capable of:	***A central processing unit (CPU)*** of at least a personal computer (PC), a cellphone, a smartphone, a laptop, or a handheld scanner, capable of:

The Google Tensor (i.e. CPU; Chipset) is considered the "brain" of the Smartphone, capable of carrying out the operational and functional instructions of the Smartphone	processing instructions to lock, unlock, or disable the lock of the communication device;	processing instructions to lock, unlock, or disable the lock of the communication device;
The Google Tensor (i.e. CPU; Chipset) is considered the "brain" of the Smartphone, capable of carrying out the operational and functional instructions of the Smartphone	processing instructions to activate a lock, unlock, or disabling lock means by engaging a vehicle with a two-way communication key-fob;	processing instructions to activate a lock, unlock, or disabling lock means by engaging a vehicle with a two-way communication key-fob;
The Google Tensor (i.e. CPU; Chipset) is considered the "brain" of the Smartphone, capable of carrying out the operational and functional instructions of the Smartphone	processing instructions to activate a start, stall, stop, or disabling means by engaging a vehicle's ignition system;	processing instructions to activate a start, stall, stop, or disabling means by engaging a vehicle's ignition system;
The Google Tensor (i.e. CPU; Chipset) is considered the "brain" of the Smartphone, capable of carrying out the operational and functional instructions of the Smartphone	processing instructions to activate a lock, unlock, or disabling lock means; a start, stall, stop, or disabling vehicle means by engaging the operational systems of the	processing instructions to activate a lock, unlock, or disabling lock means; a start, stall, stop, or disabling vehicle means by engaging the operational systems of the

	unmanned aerial vehicle;	unmanned aerial vehicle;
The Google Tensor (i.e. CPU; Chipset) is considered the “brain” of the Smartphone, capable of carrying out the operational and functional instructions of the Smartphone	processing instructions to authenticate or identify a user by at least one of biometric fingerprint recognition, biometric facial recognition, biometric iris recognition, or biometric retina recognition;	processing instructions to authenticate or identify a user by at least one of biometric fingerprint recognition, biometric facial recognition, biometric iris recognition, or biometric retina recognition;
The Google Tensor (i.e. CPU; Chipset) is considered the “brain” of the Smartphone, capable of carrying out the operational and functional instructions of the Smartphone	processing instructions to scan a senor or tag using the short-range wireless technology of radio frequency near-field communication (NFC);	processing instructions to scan a senor or tag using the short-range wireless technology of radio frequency near-field communication (NFC);
The Google Tensor (i.e. CPU; Chipset) is considered the “brain” of the Smartphone, capable of carrying out the operational and functional instructions of the Smartphone	processing instructions to monitor or detect at least one of a chemical sensor, a biological sensor, a motion sensor, a biometric sensor, a	processing instructions to monitor or detect at least one of a chemical sensor, a biological sensor, a motion sensor, a biometric sensor, a

	signature sensor, or a human sensor;	signature sensor, or a human sensor;
The Google Tensor (i.e. CPU; Chipset) is considered the "brain" of the Smartphone, capable of carrying out the operational and functional instructions of the Smartphone	processing instructions to monitor or detect for at least one of chemical agent, biological agent, radiological agent, nuclear agent, or explosive agent, weapons of mass destruction (WMDs);	processing instructions to monitor or detect for at least one of chemical agent, biological agent, radiological agent, nuclear agent, or explosive agent, weapons of mass destruction (WMDs);
The Google Tensor (i.e. CPU; Chipset) is considered the "brain" of the Smartphone, capable of carrying out the operational and functional instructions of the Smartphone	processing instructions received through at least one of a Bluetooth, a Wi-Fi, a satellite, a global positioning system (GPS), or a cellular transmission;	processing instructions received through at least one of a Bluetooth, a Wi-Fi, a satellite, a global positioning system (GPS), or a cellular transmission;
The Google Tensor (i.e. CPU; Chipset) is considered the "brain" of the Smartphone, capable of carrying out the operational and functional instructions of the Smartphone	processing instructions to connect the communication device to the internet or internet-of-things (IoTs) platform to sync, to at least one of a building's computer or security system, a vehicle's computer	processing instructions to connect the communication device to the internet or internet-of-things (IoTs) platform to sync, to at least one of a building's computer or security system, a vehicle's computer

	or security system, a lock, a detection device, or another communication device; and,	or security system, a lock, a detection device, or another communication device; and,
The Google Tensor (i.e. CPU; Chipset) is considered the "brain" of the Smartphone, capable of carrying out the operational and functional instructions of the Smartphone	whereupon, the communication device is capable of processing instructions for operational and functional execution, and is capable of providing feedback of the execution, and storing the feedback into memory.	whereupon, the central processing unit (CPU) of the communication device is capable of processing instructions for operational and functional execution, and is capable of providing feedback of the execution, and storing the feedback into memory.

Judge Rita F. Lin and Google completely ignored Golden's claim that Google's Tensor, Tensor 2, and Tensor 3 CPU/Chipset allegedly infringes independent claims 4, 5, & 6 of Golden's '287, and independent claim 11, and dependent claims 12-20 of Golden's '619 patent.

Dismissing the case without a jury trial to rule on Golden's claim that the Google Tensor Series CPU/Chipset allegedly infringes Golden patents is a clear-cut indication that Judge Rita F, Lin is bias in favor of Google and against Golden.

In the current case *Golden v. Google* LLC, N.D.Cal. Case 3:22-cv-05246-RFL Document 68 Filed 04/03/24, Judge Rita F. Lin outright lies when she says, "Golden does not allege that Google directly infringe the patents-in-suit". Golden claim Google directly infringed before Judge Rita F. Lin separated the Google phone from any means of detecting CBRN&E. Upon separation, Golden preceded to show how the Google phones 'contribute' to the infringement.

> "Liability for [] contributory infringement is dependent upon the existence of direct infringement," and "[t]here can be no [] contributory infringement without an underlying act of direct infringement." *Linear Tech. Corp. v. Impala Linear Corp.*, 379 F.3d 1311, 1326 (Fed. Cir. 2004)... "However, Golden does not allege that Google, [] directly infringed the patents-in-suit."... "To the contrary, Golden concedes that there was no such direct infringement" ... "the FAC lacks factual allegations regarding Google's knowledge of the patents-in-suit and patent infringement." *Golden v. Google* N.D.Cal. Case 3:22-cv-05246-RFL Document 68 Filed 04/03/24. [Order Granting Google's Motion to Dismiss]

Following are numbered excerpts taken from Golden's amended complaint in *Golden v. Google* N.D.Cal. Case 3:22-cv-05246-RFL

Document 42 Filed 08/23/23. Golden submits the excerpts as evidence Judge Rita F. Lin is lying when she says, "Golden does not allege that Google, [] directly infringed the patents-in-suit"... and "Golden concedes that there was no such direct infringement":

> Pursuant to the Court Order filed on 08/10/23 Dkt. 41 in *Larry Golden v, Google LLC,* Case No. 4:22-cv-05246-HSG, Plaintiff is submitting this amended ***complaint against Google LLC for alleged direct infringement,*** induced and contributory infringement, joint infringement, and willful infringement of Plaintiff's United States Patent Nos. 10,984,619 ('619 Patent), 10,163,287 ('287 Patent), 9,589,439 ('439 Patent), and 9,096,189 ('189 Patent).
>
> 1. On information and belief, Google is incorporated in the State of Delaware with a principal place of business at 1600 Amphitheatre Parkway, Mountain View, CA 94043 and does business in this judicial district by, among other things, committing jointly, ***directly,*** and/or indirectly the tort of ***literal patent infringement or infringement under the "doctrine of equivalents"*** giving rise to this complaint. Google may be served at its principal place of business at 1600 Amphitheatre Parkway, Mountain View, CA 94043.
>
> 2. Google LLC is one of the largest technology companies in the world and conducts product sales, and online search operations in the District of South Carolina. ***Google LLC directly,*** jointly, and/or indirectly distributes, markets, offers to sell, sells, and/or imports the infringing Google Pixel Series

of smartphones, Google Tensor CPU, and Google Android Operating Systems.

23. In the Federal Circuit's language, "a detailed claim chart mapping features of an accused product, the Google Pixel 5 Smartphone, to independent claims from U.S. Patent Nos. 10,163,287, 9,589,439, and 9,069,189", indicates a determination has been made on ***direct infringement, either literally or under the doctrine of equivalents.***

77. On information and belief, Google is jointly, ***directly,*** indirectly and/or under the 'doctrine of equivalents', infringing at least independent claim 11 of the '619 patent. ***The alleged infringing products are: Google Pixel 6a, 7, 7a, 7 Pro & Fold smartphones.***

As set forth in Golden's preliminary infringement contentions, Google is making, using, offering for sale, selling and/or importing Plaintiff's CMDC device have ***at a minimum directly infringed*** the '619 patent and Google is thereby liable for infringement of the '619 patent pursuant to 35 U.S.C. § 271. Google have caused damage to Golden, which infringement and damage will continue unless and until Google is enjoined.

81. On information and belief, Google is jointly, ***directly,*** indirectly and/or under the 'doctrine of equivalents', infringing at least independent claim 5 of the '287 patent. ***The alleged infringing products are: Google Pixel 6a, 7, 7a, 7 Pro & Fold smartphones.***

As set forth in Golden's preliminary infringement contentions, Google is making, using, offering for sale, selling and/or importing Plaintiff's CMDC device have ***at a minimum directly infringed*** the '287 patent and Google is thereby liable for infringement of the '287 patent pursuant to 35 U.S.C. § 271. Google have caused damage to Golden, which infringement and damage will continue unless and until Google is enjoined.

85. On information and belief, Google is jointly, ***directly,*** indirectly and/or under the 'doctrine of equivalents', infringing at least independent claims 19 and 23 of the '439 patent. ***The alleged infringing products are: Google Pixel 6a, 7, 7a, 7 Pro & Fold smartphones.***

As set forth in Golden's preliminary infringement contentions, Google is making, using, offering for sale, selling and/or importing Plaintiff's CMDC device have ***at a minimum directly infringed*** the '439 patent and Google is thereby liable for infringement of the '439 patent pursuant to 35 U.S.C. § 271. Google have caused damage to Golden, which infringement and damage will continue unless and until Google is enjoined.

89 On information and belief, Google is jointly, ***directly,*** indirectly and/or under the 'doctrine of equivalents', infringing claims 1 & 7 of the '189 patent. ***The alleged infringing products are: Google Pixel 6a, 7, 7a, 7 Pro & Fold smartphones.***

As set forth in Golden's preliminary infringement contentions that Google is making, using, offering for sale, selling and/or importing Plaintiff's CMDC device ***have at a minimum directly infringed*** the '189 patent and Google is thereby liable for infringement of the '189 patent pursuant to 35 U.S.C. § 271. Google have caused damage to Golden, which infringement and damage will continue unless and until Google is enjoined.

CHAPTER SEVEN

GOLDEN ALLEGES JUDGE RITA F. LIN CONSPIRED WITH GOOGLE TO MAKE A PARTICULAR RULING

Golden alleges Google challenged Judge Rita F. Lin to join an already established conspiracy to ensure Blacks and/or African American inventors, in a judicial system of systemic and structural racism, do not prevail at suing the Federal Government or any of the multi-billion-dollar companies who relies on the Government to treat Blacks and/or African American inventors unfairly.

Co-conspirator Google has aligned itself with the intent of the already established conspiracy to separate the patented combinations of Golden's inventions before introducing the intent to "separate and then destroy" any and all possibility of Golden being able to persuade the presiding Judge not to join the already established conspiracy.

Time and time again the Judges, including Judge Rita F. Lin, conduct is prejudicial to the effective and expeditious administration of the business of the courts. There's no law, or pending law, that Golden is aware of that allow Judges to add an inventive step to an already issued patent. The inventive step in this current case is, "the phone is modified by a third-party to function".

Rule 4 | Misconduct and Disability Definitions

(a) Misconduct Generally. Cognizable Misconduct is conduct prejudicial to the effective and expeditious administration of the business of the courts. Cognizable misconduct includes, but is not limited to, the following:

(3) Discrimination. Cognizable misconduct includes intentional discrimination on the basis of race, color, sex, gender, gender identity, pregnancy, sexual orientation, religion, national origin, age, or disability;

[A]n allegation that a judge conspired with a prosecutor to make a particular ruling is not merits-related, even though it "relates" to a ruling in a colloquial sense. Such an allegation attacks the propriety of conspiring with the prosecutor and goes beyond a challenge to the correctness — "the merits" — of the ruling itself. An allegation that the judge ruled against the complainant because the complainant is a member of a particular racial or ethnic group, or because the judge dislikes the complainant personally, is also not merits-related. Such an allegation attacks the propriety of arriving at rulings with an illicit or improper motive. An allegation that a judge treated litigants, [], or others in a demonstrably egregious and hostile manner is also not merits-related.

In this case, *Larry Golden v. Google LLC*, N.D.Cal. Case 3:22-cv-05246-RFL, Golden presented as Exhibit H of the Amended Complaint, Dkt 41; Filed 08/23/23 *"HazMat/CBRNE Mobile Apps Application Note: July 2013"* – P ages 56-71 of 125.

Golden presented this document as evidence the Google phone is not modified; and, does not need to be modified by a third-party in order to perform in an infringing manor. The software apps are developed to conform with an open-source code Google issues with each version of its Google android operating system software. Following are excerpts from the document Judge Rita F. Lin should have considered before joining the Defendant [Google], as a co-conspirator in an already established conspiracy:

- "Hazardous material (HazMat) and chemical, biological, radiological, nuclear, and explosive (CBRNE) incidents occur when substances such as toxic chemicals, biological agents, radiological or nuclear materials, or explosives pose a threat to life, property, and/or the environment." ...

- "Software applications installed on mobile devices, such as smartphones and tablets, can be useful to emergency responders, humanitarian groups, and the public. The use of these software applications, commonly called mobile apps, can improve situational awareness for the emergency responder during a HazMat/CBRNE incident"...

- "A mobile app is similar to software installed on a personal computer, but it is developed for a mobile device operating system (OS) such as [Google] Android, Apple® iOS®, BlackBerry®, or Windows® Mobile. These apps are able to integrate with other features of a mobile device, enabling them to capitalize on the functionality of global positioning system (GPS) technology, e-mail, a built-in camera, and a notification system."

- HazMat/CBRNE mobile apps can use GPS data to help responders identify access routes to an incident. An example of this type of GPS mobile app is Navfree, which allows users to access maps with or without a data connection. Other features include turn-by-turn directions, spoken instructions, and address search. Navfree is available for Apple iOS, [Google] Android, and Windows.

procurement decisions. Located within the Science and Technology Directorate (S&T) of DHS, the Emergency Response Guide (ERG) 2012 mobile app provides information to help manage a HazMat/CBRNE incident ... standard HazMat cargo signage can be quickly the SAVER

Program conducts objective assessments and validations on commercial equipment and systems and provides those results along with other relevant equipment information to the emergency response community in an operationally useful form. SAVER provides information on equipment that falls within the categories listed in the DHS Authorized Equipment List (AEL). The SAVER Program mission includes: • Conducting impartial, practitioner-relevant, operationally oriented assessments and validations of emergency responder equipment; and • Providing information, in the form of knowledge products, that enables decision-makers and emergency responders to better select, procure, use, and maintain emergency responder equipment. Information provided by the SAVER Program will be shared nationally with the responder community, providing a life- and cost-saving asset to DHS, as well as to Federal, state, and local responders. The SAVER Program is supported by a network of Technical Agents who perform assessment and validation activities. Further, SAVER focuses primarily on two main questions for the emergency responder community: "What equipment is available?" and "How does it perform?" As a SAVER Program Technical Agent, the Space and Naval Warfare Systems Center (SPAWARSYSCEN) Atlantic has been tasked to provide expertise and analysis on key subject areas, including communications, sensors, security, weapon detection, and surveillance, among others. In support of this tasking, SPAWARSYSCEN Atlantic developed this application note to provide emergency responders with information on commercially available HazMat/CBRNE mobile apps. HazMat/CBRNE mobile apps fall under AEL reference number 04AP-06-CBRN: Software, CBRNE/Commercial Chemical/Hazard.

- identified with the aid of the ERG mobile app. The ERG mobile app is available for Apple iOS and [Google] Android.

- Radiological tools can … calculate the mass and volume of radiological material based on its corresponding activity … Mobile radiation emergency medical management (Mobile REMM) is an example of a radiological mobile app tool that helps diagnose radiation exposure and determines the proper treatment during radiological or nuclear emergencies. Mobile REMM is available for Apple iOS and [Google] Android.

- Explosives tools can provide information that is helpful to emergency responders in an IED or homemade explosive (HME) incident … Alluviam LLC's HazMasterG3® mobile app provides tactical decision support for threat identification and response. Capabilities include: identification of unknown threats whether chemical, radiation or IED/HME; calculation of standoff distances and blast effects; location of hidden labs; and calculation of improvised nuclear device stand-off distances, stay-times, and fatalities.

HazMasterG3 is available for Apple iOS, [Google] Android, Blackberry, and Windows.

- Currently, there are no universally recognized standards and regulations governing mobile app development.

Upon information and belief in the information presented above, Golden alleged that the defendant Google induced infringement; thereby, causing direct infringement with its Android Open-Source Operating System under 35 U.S.C. § 271(b). Golden alleged Google actively encouraged the DoD/DTRA and Draper Laboratory Inc.'s infringement, knowing that the acts they induced constituted patent infringement, and their encouraging acts actually ***resulted*** in direct patent infringement.

In *Power Integrations, Inc. v. Fairchild Semiconductor Int'l, Inc.*, the Federal Circuit considered whether proof of induced infringement requires proof that the encouragement of infringement was successfully communicated to the direct infringer and actually ***resulted*** in direct infringement. However, *Fairchild* claimed there was no evidence that it encouraged its accused chips to be incorporated into products ... with the specific intent to induce infringement.

The court disagreed, noting that *Fairchild* was involved in activities related to the use of its products ... Fairfield [Google] designed its products [same as Google Android Open-Source Operating System] to meet certain [] standards, provided demonstration boards containing the infringing chips [open-source platform] to customers and potential customers in the United States, and maintained a technical support center in the United States that provided support to customers based in the United States."

Golden must prove the inducement ***resulted*** in direct infringement, not that the inducement was of a product that already directly infringes. According to the evidence presented in this case as Exhibit H, *"HazMat/CBRNE Mobile Apps Application Note: July 2013"*; the Google Android operating system inducement resulted in direct infringement. Therefore, it doesn't matter if the inducement, which resulted in direct infringement, came about by way of modification, adaptation, or codifying. The direct infringement is already done. *Larry Golden v. Google LLC*, N.D.Cal. Case 3:22-cv-05246-RFL Amended Complaint, Dkt 42-2 Filed 08/23/23.

Golden disclosed this information to Judge Rita F. Lin but she seems to be so blinded by prejudice, discrimination, racism, bias, and her need to fulfill her obligations as a co-conspirator in an already established conspiracy, she just could not see the hand writing on the wall that was right in front of her: The following was retrieved from the Amended Complaint, Dkt. 42.

> 49. Example: Plaintiff owns three (3) of the four (4) essential components for Google's smartphone sensing device. The host device smartphone; the central processing unit (CPU), and the smartphones camera used for CBR sensing. The only component Plaintiff have not directly written a patent claim

on, but is covered in Plaintiff's patent specifications as a "transceiver" is the operating system.

The ATAK-CBRN plugins software is built on Google's Android Open-Source Operating System (OS). The OS is responsible for managing both software and hardware components. All computer programs and apps require an operating system to do any work. Yet the OS is not the central processing unit (CPU). Plaintiff's patented CPU serves as the smartphones brain, and the OS serves as the brain's conscience.

Android is an open-source operating system for mobile devices and a corresponding open-source project led by Google. The Android Open-Source Project (AOSP) repository offer the information and source code needed to create custom variants (i.e., ATAK is built on the Android operating system) of the Android OS, port devices and accessories to the Android platform, and ensure devices meet the compatibility requirements that keep the Android ecosystem a healthy and stable environment for millions of users.

Google oversees the development of the core Android open-source platform and works to create robust developer and user communities. For the most part, the Android source code is licensed under the permissive Apache License 2.0. Google chose the Apache 2.0 license because it encourages widespread Android software adoption. Google has committed the professional engineering resources necessary to ensure that Android is a fully competitive *software* platform.

Larry Golden v. Google LLC, N.D.Cal. Case 3:22-cv-05246-RFL Amended Complaint, Dkt 42-2 Filed 08/23/23

ATAK (built on the Android operating system) With DTRA ... ATAK includes chemical, biological, radiological, and nuclear (CBRN) plug-ins. The Defense Threat Reduction Agency (DTRA) CBRN ISA: Seamlessly integrates information and control of multiple sensors into a single dashboard, making it easier to detect CBRN threats and monitor a warfighter's vitals https://thelastmile. gotennapro.com/four-useful-atak-app-plugins/

Both Draper ATAK-CIV and DoD DTRA ATAK-MIL include chemical, biological, radiological, and nuclear (CBRN) plug-ins. Golden has demonstrated throughout the complaint how Google actively encouraged the infringement; and how Google knew that the acts they were doing constituted infringement; and as a result, Google actuated direct patent infringement by those encouraging acts. Golden's evidence proves the inducement resulted in direct infringement, not that the inducement was of a product that already directly infringes.

Draper Laboratory, Inc. designed a CBRN Plugin to enable users to integrate CBRN sensors into TAK, collect CBRN sensor data, display it on a map and livestream it across the TAK network to other users. CBRN plugins for ATAK, are operational in the field.

iTAK	ATAK				WinTAK	
Apple iPhone 12 Smartphone	**Google Pixel 5 Smartphone**	**Samsung Galaxy S21 Smartphone**	**LG V60 ThinQ 5G**	**Asus / Qualcomm Smartphone for Snapdragon Insiders**	**Samsung Galaxy Book2 Pro 360 [PC Mode or Tablet Mode]**	**HP ZBook Fury 15.6 Inch G8 Mobile Workstation PC**
					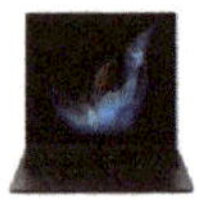	
Chipset: Apple A14 Bionic (5 nm). **CPU**: Hexa-core (2x3.1 GHz Firestorm + 4x1.8 GHz Icestorm).	**Chipset:** Qualcomm Snapdragon 765G **CPU**: Octa-core (1 × 2.4 GHz Kryo 475 Prime	**Chipset:** Qualcomm SM8350 **CPU:** Octa-core (1x2.84 GHz Cortex-X1 & 3x2.42 GHz	**Chipset**: Qualcomm SM8250 **CPU:** Octa-core (1x2.84 GHz Cortex-A77 & 3x2.42 GHz	**Chipset:** Qualcomm SM8350 **CPU:** Octa-core (1x2.84 GHz Cortex-X1 & 3x2.42 GHz	**CPU**: Intel® Core™ i5-1235U / Intel® Core™ i7-1255U. Processor Speed 1.3GHz / 1.7 GHz.	**CPU**: 11th Generation Intel® Xeon® W-11955M vPro® with Intel® UHD Graphics
OS: Apple iOS 14.1, upgradable to iOS 16.1	**OS**: Google Android 11, upgradable to Android 13	**OS**: Google Android 11, upgradable to Android 13	**OS**: Google Android 10, upgradable to Android 13	**OS**: Google Android 11	**OS**: Preinstalled Microsoft Windows 11	**OS**: Preinstalled Microsoft Windows 11 Pro2

CBRNE PLUGIN S Draper Laborator y, Inc	**CBRNE PLUGIN S** Draper Laborator y, Inc	**CBRNE PLUGIN S** Draper Laborator y, Inc	**CBRN E PLUGI NS** Draper Laborato ry, Inc	**CBRNE PLUGIN S** Draper Laborator y, Inc	**CBRNE PLUGI NS** Draper Laborato ry, Inc	**CBRNE PLUGIN S** Draper Laborator y, Inc

Larry Golden v. Google LLC Case 3:22-cv-05246-RFL Dkt. 42-2 Filed 08/23/23 Page 2 of 120

Claim Chart of Induced Infringement [DTRA ATAK-MILITARY and Draper's ATAK-CIVILIAN; Contributory Infringement of Google's Pixel 6a, 7, 7a, 7 Pro, and Fold Smartphones

DRAPER'S ATAK-CIVILIAN & DoD/DTRA ATAK-MILITARY	Patent #: 9,589,439; Independent Claim 19	Patent #: 9,096,189; Independent Claim 7
 Both Draper ATAK-CIV and DoD DTRA ATAK-MIL include chemical, biological, radiological, and nuclear (CBRN) plug-ins. Golden has demonstrated throughout the complaint how Google actively encouraged the infringement; and how Google knew that the acts they were doing constituted	A multi-sensor detection system for detecting at least one explosive, nuclear, contraband, chemical, biological, human, radiological agent, or compound, comprising:	A multi-sensor detection system for detecting at least one explosive, nuclear, contraband, chemical, biological, human, or radiological agents and compounds, comprising:

infringement; and as a result, Google actuated direct patent infringement by those encouraging acts. Golden's evidence proves the inducement ***resulted*** in direct infringement, not that the inducement was of a product that already directly infringes.		
ATAK-CIVILIAN Draper Laboratory, Inc. designed a CBRN Plugin to enable users to integrate CBRN sensors into TAK, collect CBRN sensor data, display it on a map and livestream it across the TAK network to other users. CBRN plugins for ATAK, are operational in the field. **ATAK-MILITARY** ATAK (built on the Android operating system) With DTRA ... ATAK includes chemical, biological, radiological, and nuclear (CBRN) plug-ins. The Defense Threat Reduction Agency (DTRA) CBRN ISA: Seamlessly integrates information and control of multiple sensors into a single dashboard, making it easier to detect CBRN threats and monitor a warfighter's vitals https://thelastmile. gotennapro.com/four-useful-atak-app-plugins/	a plurality of sensors for detecting at least one chemical, biological, radiological, explosive, nuclear, human, or contraband agent or compound, capable of being disposed within, on, upon or adjacent a multi-sensor detection device;	a plurality of sensors for detecting at least one chemical, biological, radiological, explosive, nuclear, human or contraband agents and compounds and capable of being disposed within, on, upon or adjacent a multi sensor detection device;
Pursuant to 35 U.S.C. § 271(c), Google has contributed an element(s) [at least that of Google Pixel 6a, 7, 7a, 7 Pro, or Fold] to the alleged infringing ATAK CBRNE Plugins of Draper Laboratory, Inc. and the Defense Threat Reduction Agency (DTRA). Google is contributing to the infringement of independent claim 19 of Golden's '439 patent, and independent claim 7 of Golden's '189 patent. ATAK (including CivTAK) is an Android smartphone [i.e., Google smartphone]	monitoring equipment comprising at least one of a computer, personal computer (PC), laptop, notebook PC, handheld, cell phone, personal digital assistant (PDA) or smart phone for at least one of a receipt or	monitoring equipment comprising at least one of plurality product groups based on the categories of a computer, laptop, notebook, PC, handheld, cell phone, PDA or smart phone for the receipt and transmission of

geospatial infrastructure and situational awareness app https://www.civtak.org/atak-about/. ATAK can be downloaded to a phone, tablet, or handheld device. ATAK-MIL is a government-off-the-shelf app for Android smartphones. The mobile broadband 4G LTE connection is able to facilitate the data throughput required for the operation of the ATAK. https://apps. dtic.mil/sti/pdfs/ AD1069441.pdf Golden has alleged Joint or Divided infringement between Google and Draper; and, Google and DTRA, because no single party carried out all the steps of Golden's patented inventions, that would constitute infringement.	transmission of signals therebetween;	signals therebetween;
Google Pixel 6a, 7, 7a, 7 Pro, and Fold smartphones connects to a cell tower or base station via radio waves, and that tower is usually physically connected to the infrastructure to send that data wherever it needs to go. Draper designed a chemical, biological, radiological and nuclear (CBRN) Plugin to enable users to integrate CBRN sensors into TAK, collect CBRN sensor data, display it on a map and livestream it across the TAK network to other users. CBRN plugins for ATAK, WinTAK and WebTAK are operational in the field. https://www.draper.com/explore-solutions/tak	at least one cell phone tower interconnected to the monitoring equipment for sending signals thereto and receiving signals therefrom or at least one satellite capable of transmitting signals to the monitoring equipment;	at least one cell phone tower interconnected to the monitoring equipment for sending signals thereto and receiving signals therefrom or at least one satellite capable of transmitting signals to the monitoring equipment;
The Android-based Google Pixel 6a, 7, 7a, 7 Pro, and Fold smartphones now contained integrated satellite on-the move capability, on-the-move mapping solutions, and a commercial laser range finder that	at least one satellite or at least one cell phone tower capable of signal	at least one satellite or at least one cell phone tower capable of signal

significantly expanded the end-user range data flow and functionality. The Primary, Alternate, Contingency, and Emergency (PACE) communications architectures established was: • Primary communications structure (P): ATAK—4G/LTE; Antenna: international [] satellite (INMARSAT) https://apps. dtic.mil/sti/pdfs/ AD1069441.pdf	communication between the multi-sensor detection device and the monitoring equipment;	communication between the multi sensor detection device and the monitoring equipment;
The internet connection is shared by many ATAK functions on the Google Pixel 6a, 7, 7a, 7 Pro, and Fold smartphone such as internet browsing, receiving email messages and installing apps. Wi-Fi is a method for devices such as the Google Pixel 6a, 7, 7a, 7 Pro, or Fold smartphones to connect wirelessly to the Internet using radio waves.	at least one internet connection capable of communication between the multi-sensor detection device and the monitoring equipment;	at least one internet connection capable of communication between the multi sensor detection device and the monitoring equipment;
Sit(x) is a commercial Server-as-a-Service solution based on the TAK platform developed by PAR Government for the U.S. Defense & Intelligence Community. Sit(x) has real-time communication and information sharing. With Sit(x), individuals and teams can communicate via personal computers and handheld mobile [Google smartphone] devices by voice or text. They can share real-time full-motion video (FMV), airborne/drone imagery, GPS locations, photos, and satellite imagery. Fully secure and compatible with ATAK, WinTAK, and iTAK. Sit(x) accessed via free downloadable gateway apps.	whereupon a signal sent to a receiver of the multi-sensor detection device from a satellite; or to a cell phone tower; or through at least one of a short-range radio frequency or a long-range radio frequency; causes a signal to be sent to the monitoring equipment that includes at least one of location data or sensor data;	whereupon a signal sent to a receiver of the multi sensor detection device from a satellite; or to a cell phone tower; or through short and/or long-range radio frequency; causes a signal to be sent to the monitoring equipment that includes location data and sensor data;

The '439 & '189 patent specs: Product grouping (PG) 1 (storage & transportation); PG 2 (sensors); PG 3 (detector case; modified and adapted); PG 4 (monitoring & communication devices); PG 5 (communication methods); PG 6 (biometrics); and, PG 7 (authorized person)	wherein the monitoring equipment or multi-sensor detection device receives a signal via any of one or more products of any product grouping categories;	wherein the monitoring equipment or multi sensor detection device receives a signal via any of one or more products listed in any of the plurality of product grouping categories;
The Android-based [Google] Google Pixel 6a, 7, 7a, 7 Pro, and Fold smartphones now contained integrated satellite ... Wi-Fi is a method for devices such as the Google Pixel 6a, 7, 7a, 7 Pro, or Fold smartphone to connect wirelessly to the Internet using radio waves... The internet connection is shared by many ATAK functions on the Google Pixel 6a, 7, 7a, 7 Pro, or Fold smartphone such as internet browsing, receiving email messages; installing apps... The Google Pixel 6a, 7, 7a, 7 Pro, or Fold smartphone connects to a cell tower or base station via radio waves, and that tower is usually physically connected to the infrastructure to send that data wherever it needs to go.	wherein at least one of a satellite connection, Bluetooth connection, WiFi connection, internet connection, radio frequency (RF) connection, cellular connection, broadband connection, long range radio frequency connection, or short-range radio frequency (RF) connection is capable of signal communication with the transmitter, a receiver of the monitoring equipment, the multi-sensor	wherein at least one satellite connection, Bluetooth connection, WiFi connection, internet connection, radio frequency (RF) connection, cellular connection, broadband connection, long and short-range radio frequency (RF) connection is capable of signal communication with the transmitter and the receiver of the monitoring equipment or multi sensor detection device and transceivers

	detection device, or transceivers of the products;	of the products;
BIOMETRICS: Biometric factors allow for secure authentication on the Android platform. The Android framework includes face and fingerprint biometric authentication. Android can be customized to support other forms of biometric authentication (such as Iris). ATAK (including CivTAK) is an Android smartphone [i.e., Google smartphone] geospatial infrastructure and situational awareness app https://www.civtak.org/atak-about/. ATAK can be downloaded to a phone, tablet, or handheld device. (Google Pixel 6a, 7, 7a, 7 Pro, or Fold smartphones)	wherein the monitoring equipment is equipped with a biometric lock disabler that incorporates at least one of a fingerprint recognition, voice recognition, face recognition, hand geometry, retina scan, iris scan or signature such that the monitoring device that is at least one of the computer, the laptop, the notebook, the PC, the handheld, the cell phone, the PDA, or the smart phone is locked by the biometric lock disabler to prevent unauthorized use;	wherein the monitoring equipment is equipped with a biometric lock disabler that incorporates at least one of a fingerprint recognition, voice recognition, face recognition, hand geometry, retina scan, iris scan and signature such that the monitoring device that is at least one of the computer, the laptop, the notebook, the PC, the handheld, the cell phone, the PDA, or the smart phone is locked by the biometric lock disabler to prevent unauthorized use;
The Android-based [Google] Google Pixel 6a, 7, 7a, 7 Pro, and Fold smartphones now contained integrated satellite ... Wi-Fi is a method for devices such as the Google Pixel 6a, 7, 7a, 7 Pro, or Fold	wherein the only type or types of communication with the transmitter and the receiver of the	wherein the only type or types of communication with the transmitter and the receiver of the

smartphone to connect wirelessly to the Internet using radio waves... The internet connection is shared by many ATAK functions on the Google Pixel 6a, 7, 7a, 7 Pro, or Fold smartphone such as internet browsing, receiving email messages; installing apps... The Google Pixel 6a, 7, 7a, 7 Pro, or Fold smartphone connects to a cell tower or base station via radio waves, and that tower is usually physically connected to the infrastructure to send that data wherever it needs to go.	communication device and transceivers of the products is a type or types selected from the group consisting of satellite, Bluetooth, WiFi, internet, radio frequency (RF), cellular, broadband, long range radio frequency, and short-range radio frequency (RF).	communication device and transceivers of the products is a type or types selected from the group consisting of satellite, Bluetooth, WiFi, internet, radio frequency (RF), cellular, broadband, and long and short-range radio frequency (RF).

CHAPTER EIGHT

JUDGE RITA F. LIN OUTRIGHT LIED WHEN SHE STATED, "AS THE COMPLAINT DID NOT ALLEGE THAT THE GOOGLE SMARTPHONES *THEMSELVES* INFRINGED ON THE PATENTS"

To be clear, Golden is not arguing the merits of the case, Golden is simply asking the question, why is it Judge Rita F. Lin is willing to go so far as to outright lie about the merits of the case? To outright lie about the case, obviously means the Judge has a personal bias against Golden as a Black and/or African American. It also means the Judge is willing to go to any length—lying on an official document—to fulfill her obligation as a co-conspirator in an already established conspiracy of systemic and structural racism within the judicial system.

As stated earlier, the reason Golden filed the case is because the Federal Circuit in *Larry Golden v. Google LLC*; Case No. 22-1267 reversed and remanded the alleged direct infringement of Google's Pixel 5 smartphone, "Mr. Golden's complaint includes a detailed claim chart mapping features of an accused product, the Google Pixel 5 Smartphone, to independent claims from U.S. Patent Nos. 10,163,287, 9,589,439, and 9,069,189 ... It [claim chart] attempts [] to map claim limitations to infringing product features, and it does so in a relatively straightforward manner ...".

But yet, Judge Rita F. Lin writes in an official document, "[a]s the complaint did not allege that the Google smartphones *themselves* infringed on the patents, Golden failed to allege direct infringement".

> As the complaint did not allege that the Google smartphones *themselves* infringed on the patents, Golden failed to allege direct infringement. (Id. at 6.) As liability for indirect infringement is dependent on the existence of direct infringement, Golden also failed to allege indirect infringement. (Id. at 7.)"

Also, Judge Rita F. Lin's ignorance does not equate to a ruling on the merits. If the Judge has access to the information and is capable of interpreting or comprehending the information but rules away from what she knows to be true, then it's a lie. In this case the Judge was provided all the information she needed to make an informed decision on the merits, or at the very least enough information that upon discovery Google can be charged with "exercising the requisite 'direction or control' over the others" in a cause of "joint infringement".

> Golden fails to allege joint infringement. "A claim of joint infringement . . . requires pleading facts sufficient to allow a reasonable inference that all steps of the claimed method are performed and either (1) one party exercises the requisite 'direction or control' over the others' performance []" *Lyda v. CBS Corp.*, 838 F.3d 1331, 1339 (Fed. Cir. 2016) ... It appears that Golden is alleging joint infringement by Google and Draper Laboratory, or possibly by Google and DTRA, but there are no factual allegations regarding the degree of control that Google had over Draper Laboratory or DTRA, or vice versa...

Golden has repeatedly, over and over again, provided Judge Rita F. Lin with an abundance of evidence proving Google has a lot more than just a degree of control. First, Google is more than just a distributor, Google makes, uses, sells, and offers for sell the Google Pixel Smartphone Series; second, Google owns the Google Tensor CPU/Chipset Series, that is considered the "brains" of the smartphone devices capable of carrying out the operational and functional instructions of the devices; and third, Google owns the Android Open-Source Operating System Platform. Golden has explained in great detail, because the DoD DTRA ATAK software is built on the Android Open-Source Operating System, the level of degree this system has on the control of integrating software and software. Golden provided an entire section to this fact in the original complaint:

SENSOR TYPES SUPPORTED BY THE "*ANDROID*" PLATFORM

Type Accelerometer	Hardware	Measures the acceleration force in m/s^2 that is applied to a device on all three physical axes (x, y, and z), including the force of gravity.	Motion detection (shake, tilt, etc.).
Type Ambient Temperature	Hardware	Measures the ambient room temperature in degrees Celsius (°C). See note below.	Monitoring air temperatures.
Type Gravity	Software or Hardware	Measures the force of gravity in m/s^2 that is applied to a device on all three physical axes (x, y, z).	Motion detection (shake, tilt, etc.).
Type Gyroscope	Hardware	Measures a device's rate of rotation in rad/s around each of the three physical axes (x, y, and z).	Rotation detection (spin, turn, etc.).
Type Light	Hardware	Measures the ambient light level (illumination) in lx.	Controlling screen brightness.
Type Linear Acceleration	Software or Hardware	Measures the acceleration force in m/s^2 that is applied to a device on all three physical axes (x, y, and z), excluding the force of gravity.	Monitoring acceleration along a single axis.
Type Magnetic Field	Hardware	Measures the ambient geomagnetic field for all three physical axes (x, y, z) in μT.	Creating a compass.
Type Orientation	Software	Measures degrees of rotation that a device makes around all three physical axes (x, y, z). As of API level 3 you can obtain the inclination matrix and rotation matrix for a device by	Determining device position.

		using the gravity sensor and the geomagnetic field sensor in conjunction with the get Rotation Matric () method.	
Type Pressure	Hardware	Measures the ambient air pressure in hPa or mbar.	Monitoring air pressure changes.
Type Proximity	Hardware	Measures the proximity of an object in cm relative to the view screen of a device. This sensor is typically used to determine whether a handset is being held up to a person's ear.	Phone position during a call.
Type Relative Humidity	Hardware	Measures the relative ambient humidity in percent (%).	Monitoring dewpoint, absolute, and relative humidity.
Type Rotation Vector	Software or Hardware	Measures the orientation of a device by providing the three elements of the device's rotation vector.	Motion detection and rotation detection.
Type Temperature	Hardware	Measures the temperature of the device in degrees Celsius (°C). This sensor implementation varies across devices and this sensor was replaced with the **Type—Ambient Temperature** sensor in API Level 14	Monitoring temperatures.

- BIOMETRICS: Biometric factors allow for secure authentication on the Android platform. The Android framework includes face and fingerprint biometric authentication. Android can be customized to support other forms of biometric authentication (such as Iris).

- DISABLING LOCK MECHANISM: Google's Android operating system features a lock mechanism to secure your phone, known as pattern lock. When setting the pattern, you must drag your finger along lines on the screen between different nodes. Afterward, to unlock the phone, you'll need to replicate the pattern drawn. If you fail to solve the pattern too many times, the phone locks and cannot be unlocked without logging into the associated Google account. If you can't log in, you'll have to employ some other methods to restore control of your phone.

- CHEMICAL, BIOLOGICAL, RADIOLOGICAL, AND NUCLEAR (CBRN) DETECTION: Through collaboration and innovation, the Defense Threat Reduction Agency has integrated its powerful, hazard-awareness-and-response tools into the *Android Tactical Assault Kit (or the Android Team Awareness Kit, ATAK).* ATAK is a digital application available to warfighters throughout the DoD. Built on the Android operating system, ATAK offers warfighters geospatial mapping for situational awareness during combat — on an end-user device such as a smartphone or a tablet. With DTRA's contribution, ATAK now includes chemical, biological, radiological, and nuclear (CBRN) plug-ins.

- HEART RATE: *Android Team Awareness Kit, ATAK* provides a single interface for viewing and controlling different CBRN-sensing technologies, whether that is a wearable smartwatch that measures a warfighter's vitals (e.g., heart rate) or a device mounted on a drone to detect chemical warfare agents.

- NEAR FIELD COMMUNICATION (NFC): Pixel™, Phone by Google - Turn NFC on/off. Near Field Communication (NFC) allows the transfer of data between devices that are a few centimeters apart, typically back-to-back. NFC must be turned on for NFC-based apps (e.g., Tap to Pay) to function correctly. NFC is a set of short-range wireless technologies, typically requiring a distance of 4cm or less to initiate a connection. NFC allows you to share small payloads of data between an NFC tag and an Android-powered device, or between two Android-powered devices. Tags can range in complexity.

- WARFIGHTERS: The U.S. armed forces and their interagency and coalition partners value *Android Team Awareness Kit, ATAK* and the common operating picture it provides. DTRA continues to develop CBRN-specific plug-in capabilities to support warfighters on the battlefield.

Golden devoted an entire section in the Amended Complaint to demonstrating the degree of control that Google had over the DoD DTRA ATAK software development.

CHAPTER NINE

GOOGLE CAUSED THE INFRINGEMENT OF PLAINTIFF'S PATENTS

Android is an open-source operating system for mobile devices and a corresponding open-source project led by Google. The Android Open-Source Project (AOSP) repository offer the information and source code needed to create custom variants (i.e., ATAK is built on the Android operating system) of the Android OS, port devices and accessories to the Android platform, and ensure devices meet the compatibility requirements that keep the Android ecosystem a healthy and stable environment for millions of users.

Google oversees the development of the core Android open-source platform and works to create robust developer and user communities. For the most part, the Android source code is licensed under the permissive Apache License 2.0. Google chose the Apache 2.0 license because it encourages widespread Android software adoption. Google has committed the professional engineering resources necessary to ensure that Android is a fully competitive *software* platform.

Each platform version of Android (such as 1.5 or 8.1) has a corresponding branch in the open-source tree. The most recent branch is considered the current stable branch version. This is the branch that manufacturers port to their devices.

The Google Android *software* is first built into a system image for a device and put through various forms of certification, including government regulatory certification for the regions the phones will be deployed.

When the release is approved by the regulators and operators, the manufacturer begins mass producing devices, and Google begin releasing the source code. Simultaneous to mass production, the Google team kicks off several efforts to prepare the open-source release, that include making final API changes and updating documentation to reflect any modifications that were made during qualification testing. Google's legal team does a final sign-off to release the code into open source.

The Android Open-Source Project maintains Android software, and develops new versions. Because it's open source, this software can be used for any purpose. The function of the Android Compatibility Program is to define a baseline implementation of Android that is compatible with third-party apps [DoD/DTRA/ATAK apps] written by developers.

Devices that are Android compatible are eligible to participate in the Android ecosystem.

Google APIs are mechanisms that enable two software components [Google Android operating system software and the ATAK software that is built on the Android operating system] to communicate with each other using a set of definitions and protocols.

API stands for Application Programming Interface. In the context of APIs, the word Application refers to any software with a distinct function. Interface can be thought of as a contract of service between two applications. This contract defines how the two communicate with each other using requests and responses.

Android Team Awareness Kit, ATAK (built on the Android operating system) is a digital application available to warfighters throughout the DoD. ATAK offers warfighters geospatial mapping for situational awareness during combat — on an end-user device such as a smartphone or a tablet. With DTRA's contribution, ATAK now includes chemical, biological, radiological, and nuclear (CBRN) plug-ins.

> *Android Team Awareness Kit,* ATAK (built on the Android operating system) provides a single interface for viewing and controlling different CBRN-sensing technologies, whether that is a wearable smartwatch that measures a warfighter's vitals (e.g., heart rate) or a device mounted on a drone to detect chemical warfare agents.

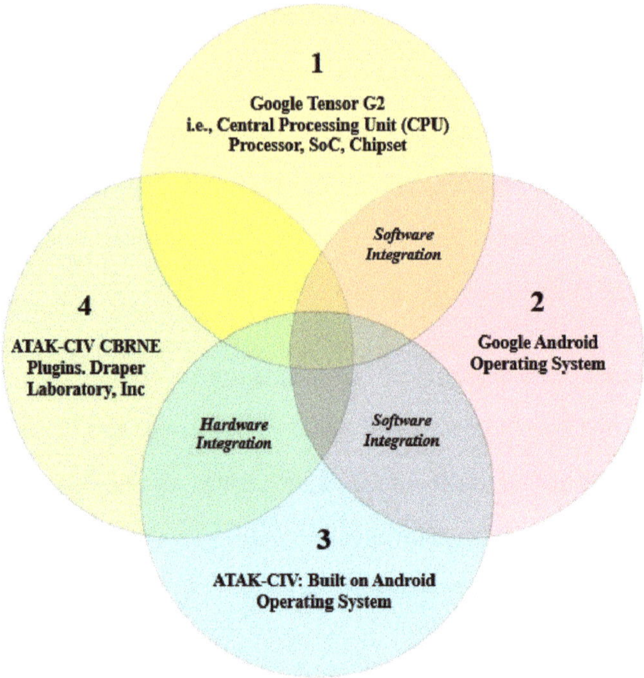

The TAK suite of tools uses plugins, allowing users to design applications specific to their mission needs. For example, ATAK can connect to sensors, satellites, drones, and smartwatches, enabling integration of valuable data from operators and team members and the environment.

Draper Laboratory, Inc. designed a CBRN Plugin to enable users to integrate CBRN sensors into TAK, collect CBRN sensor data, display it on a map and livestream it across the TAK network to other users. CBRN plugins for ATAK, are operational in the field.

Given the information above that was retrieved from both the original complaint and the amended complaint, and the information below that was retrieved from the Google website, one could say Google is very close to being entirely in control of the DoD DTRA ATAK software development for the function of Draper's CBRNE Plug-in sensors.

Google's Open-Source: Public domain and "Free for Any Use"

NOTE: Apply this label with caution. Public domain is a complex topic that requires legal analysis on a case-by-case basis. You must email and ask for a special review before you check in public domain code.

The 'unencumbered' licenses include those often referred to as "Public Domain" or "free for any use." These licenses have even fewer restrictions than licenses in the 'notice' category, but this license type should be assigned to a third-party build rule with caution, because:

- It is non-trivial to place software in the public domain. While an explicit disclaimer of copyright protection is required, that is not necessarily sufficient.
- While works of the U.S. Government are placed in the public domain, works created by contractors under government contracts may not be.

As noted at go/thirdparty/documentation#google-owned-code, The LICENSE file for Google-authored, not-yet-released code should only contain the following text: "Google owned, no external contributions." Once a project has been open sourced with an accompanying LICENSE, the project must use the LICENSE in the package rather than be treated as unencumbered and any external contributions must sign a Contributor License Agreement (see go/cla).

https://opensource.google/documentation/reference/thirdparty/licenses

Effective software supply chain management requires licensing as well as security compliance. The DTRA use of Google's open-source components and libraries to build the DTRA ATAK software knew those components are governed by Google's open-source licenses. Even one noncompliant license in the ATAK software can result in legal issues, loss of lucrative intellectual property, time-consuming remediation efforts, and delays in getting the DTRA ATAK software product to market.

Therefore, as stated earlier, Judge Rita F. Lin's reliance on the theory "the Google phones had to be modified to perform the detector/sensor function" is without merit. Google owns the phones; owns the CPUs; owns the operating systems and platform; and; Google controls the development of software built or developed on the Google Android Open-Source Operating System Platform through its licensing agreements.

The Co-conspirator Judge Rita F. Lin has a personal bias against Golden and in favor of Google, LLC.

CHAPTER TEN

JUDGE RITA F. LIN JOINS AS A CO-CONSPIRATOR QUALCOMM INCORPORATION'S CONSPIRACY

In 2008, the White-owned company Qualcomm Inc.; six other White-own companies of SeaCoast, Rhevision, Synkera, Apple, Samsung, and LG; and, one Government agency of NASA formed a conspiracy with the Department of Homeland Security (DHS) to appropriate and use Golden's patented inventions without paying just compensation.

> "[A patent] confers upon the patentee an exclusive property in the patented invention which cannot be appropriated or used by the government itself, without just compensation, any more than it can appropriate or use without compensation land which has been patented to a private purchaser." *James v. Campbell*, 104 U.S. 356, 358 (1882)

A conspiracy is traditionally defined as "an agreement between two or more persons to achieve an unlawful object or to achieve a lawful object by unlawful means." See *Douglas G. Smith, Comment, The Intracorporate Conspiracy Doctrine* and 42 U.S.C. § 1985(3): *The Original Intent,* 90 NW. U. L. REV. 1125, 1170(1996) (defining "conspiracy").

According to the Supreme Court, the plurality element of a conspiracy charge represents a "distinct evil." See *United States v. Jimenez Recio,* 537 U.S. 270, 274-75 (2003) (quoting *Salinas v. United States,* 522 U.S. 52, 65 (1997)). This stems from the idea that two people who agree to commit a crime create a more dangerous threat to society than one or both of them planning to commit the same offense independently. See *Krulewitch v. United States,* 336 U.S. 440, 448-49 (1949).

A civil conspiracy, while not criminally punishable, contains the same plurality of actors' element. See *Beye v. Bureau of Nat'l Affairs,* 477 A.2d 1197, 1206 (Md. Ct. Spec. App. 1984) (defining civil conspiracy). A civil conspiracy is defined as "a combination of two or more persons by an agreement or understanding to accomplish an unlawful act or to use unlawful means to accomplish an act not in itself illegal, with the further requirement that the act or the means employed must result in damages to the plaintiff." *Id.* (citing *Green v. Wash. Sub. San. Comm'n,* 296 A.2d 815, 824 (Md. 1970)).

Qualcomm has eluded prosecution for its illegal behavior, actions, and activities for years. Qualcomm has taken advantage of a judicial system that is plagued with systemic and structural racism; and Judges who are judicially bias toward the Government agencies and large corporations, over that of a *Pro Se* Black and/or African American litigant.

In 2008, Qualcomm was one of seven White-owned companies awarded contracts by the Dept. of Homeland Security (DHS) in the DHS S&T *Cell-All* BAA07-10 initiative, as the prime contractor responsible for developing three of Golden's, a Black and/or African American, inventions [new, improved cell phone; CBRNE sensors; and smartphone CPUs]. As long as Qualcomm was performing work for the Government under the *Cell-All* BAA07-10 initiative, Qualcomm was shielded by the DHS [Government] from infringement liability.

Golden, the Black and/or African American who owns the patent rights for the technology the DHS authorized and consented to Qualcomm et al infringing upon, was not awarded a contract or offered a licensing agreement. Qualcomm was named the prime contractor responsible for the development and assembly of three of the requested components that infringes Golden's patents, i.e., the new, improved upon, and useful cell phone, the central processing unit (CPU), and the CBRNE sensors/detectors.

Title VI, 42 U.S.C. § 2000d et seq., was enacted as part of the landmark Civil Rights Act of 1964. It prohibits the DHS, who awarded seven White-owned companies' contracts, from discriminating against Golden, on the basis of race, color or national origin, in programs and activities receiving federal financial assistance. As President Kennedy said in 1963:

"Simple justice requires that public funds, to which all taxpayers of all races [colors, and national origins] contribute, not be spent in any fashion which encourages, entrenches, subsidizes or results in racial [color or national origin] discrimination."

The DHS avoided liability because at the time, as long as one process of Golden's patented invention was made or assembled abroad, the Government (DHS) could not be held liable for direct infringement under 28 U.S.C. § 1498(a). *Zoltek III* [overturned in *Zoltek V*].

In 2014, the Dept. of Homeland Security (DHS), who was protecting Qualcomm from patent infringement liability, and the Dept. of Justice (DOJ), who was representing Qualcomm and the six other third-party White-owned companies in *Golden v. USA* case no. 13-307C; petition the Patent Trials and Appeals Board (PTAB) as "persons" not authorized to do so [*Return Mail v. U.S. Postal Service*], with three unqualified patent references that do not antedate Golden's patent(s).

The PTAB [the third Government agency to join the conspiracy], being judicially bias for the benefit of Qualcomm et al, the DHS and the DOJ, decided to institute trial against Golden, a Black and/or African American, with the three unqualified references of Astrin, Breed, and Mostov.

Qualcomm, or any of the six other White-owned companies could have petitioned the PTAB as "persons" authorized to do so. The DHS, DOJ, and PTAB have never before instituted an IPR against a White with unqualified patent references to invalidate their patents.

In 2019, the Ninth Circuit in *FTC v. Qualcomm,* reversed the opinion of the Northern District of California Court of a permanent injunction against Qualcomm. The injunction was issued to enjoin Qualcomm from charging and collecting a royalty on Golden's patented CPU Qualcomm "tied" to its cellular modem and sells as a Snapdragon chipset; and collecting a 5% running royalty on the price of Golden's patented handsets.

Senior Judge Eric Bruggink and the Court of Federal Claims who joined the conspiracy in 2013, knew the prime contractor Qualcomm for the *Cell-All* initiative was responsible for providing the CPUs "brains" of the handset devices and wanted to protect Qualcomm's illegal collecting of a "running royalty of 5% on the price of each smartphone sold". *FTC. v. Qualcomm,* 411 F. Supp. 3d 658 (N.D. Cal. 2019). District Judge Lucy H. Koh concluded Qualcomm is being unjustly enriched from its anticompetitive practices:

> "Qualcomm stopped licensing rival modem chip suppliers and instead started licensing only OEMs (i.e., Samsung, LG, Apple, Google, etc.) at a *5% running royalty on the price of each handset sold.* These licenses are called Subscriber Unit License Agreements ("SULA")"
>
> "Specifically, Qualcomm charges a 5% running royalty on handset sales for a license to Qualcomm's CDMA patent portfolio. Qualcomm's 5% royalty rate on the price of each phone sold is a species of unfair competition. The Federal

Trade Commission Act bans "unfair methods of competition" and "unfair or deceptive acts or practices."

Judge Lucy H. Koh concluded Qualcomm is being "unjustly enriched" from its anticompetitive practices of collecting a 5% running royalty on the price of each "smartphone" sold [*FTC* - "unfair methods of competition" and "unfair or deceptive acts or practices"] from the OEMs Samsung, Google, etc. Qualcomm monopolized the market on illegally collecting royalties on Golden's patented smartphone invention, thereby restraining Golden from collecting royalties from the OEMs Samsung, Google, etc. for the making, using, offering for sell, and selling of Golden's patented smartphone invention [35 U.S.C. § 271(a)].

This type of antitrust injury to Golden is of a type that the antitrust laws were intended to prevent; and Golden's injury flows from that which makes Qualcomm's acts unlawful. The District Court and Appellate Court ignored the fact that the controversy exceeds twenty dollars, and Golden's right of trial by jury is preserved [U.S. CONST. amend. VII].

The District Court and the Appellate Court, who joined the conspiracy as co-conspirators, fail to allow a trial by jury [U.S. CONST. amend. VII] upon Golden, a Black and/or African American demand, to determine if Qualcomm's illegal collection of a 5% running royalty on the price of each "smartphone" sold violates antitrust laws only [*FTC. v. Qualcomm*, 411 F. Supp. 3d 658 (N.D. Cal. 2019]; patent laws only [whoever "uses" any patented invention without authority or legal right to do so, infringes the patent—35 U.S.C. § 271(a)], or both antitrust laws and patent laws.

The DOJ and the DOE [who join the conspiracy] intervened at the Ninth Circuit against a sister agency, the *FTC*, and basically stated the only person harmed by Qualcomm's actions is a Black and/or African American patent owner. Qualcomm was made knowledgeable of Golden's IP in 2008.

In 2019, Qualcomm was notified by the co-conspirators DOJ and the U.S. Court of Federal Claims (COFC) to appear in *Golden v. USA* case no. 13-307C, but Qualcomm failed to appear. The co-conspirator DOJ proceeded to drop everything the prime contractor Qualcomm in the DHS S&T *Cell-All* BAA07-10 initiative was responsible for developing [Golden's patented new, improved cell phone; CBRNE sensors; and CPUs] just to make the case a dispute between private parties.

The co-conspirator COFC Judge, knew or should have known, the COFC does not have jurisdiction to litigate disputes between private parties [the DOJ dropped Qualcomm and the other six white-owned companies awarded contracts under the DHS S&T *Cell-All* BAA07-10 initiative and narrowed the dispute between the private parties of Golden and Apple, away from that of *Golden v. The DHS*]. Golden is not required to prove direct infringement under 35 U.S.C. § 271(a) as a predicate to proving direct infringement under 28 U.S.C. § 1498(a) *Zoltek V.*

The COFC [Government], being judicially bias in favor of the DHS and DOJ, decided to blame the Golden, a Black and/or African American, for failure to prove direct infringement under 35 U.S.C. § 271(a) as a predicate to proving direct infringement under 28 U.S.C. § 1498(a) (*Zoltek V)* and dismissed the case.

Between the years 2019 and 2022, Golden, a *Pro Se* Black and/or African American, have demanded a jury trial under the Seventh Amendment to litigate Golden's alleged patent infringement claims against Qualcomm, in the U.S. District Court for the District of South Carolina and the U.S. District Court for the Northern District of California; but, because of systemic/structural racism and judicial bias in favor of Qualcomm, Golden have been denied his Seventh Amendment right to a trial by jury. Golden's patent infringement claims against Qualcomm is an issue-of-fact tried by a jury under the Seventh Amendment.

The Due Process Clause of the Fifth Amendment generally prohibit federal governments [Judge Rita F. Lin included] from "depriving any person of [] property, without due process of law." Due process, while not "precisely defined," generally refers to a "fundamental fairness" requirement when the government [Judge Rita F. Lin included] seeks to burden an individual's property interests. According to the Supreme Court, the "touchstone" of due process is "the protection of the individual against arbitrary action of government [Judge Rita F. Lin]."

The Supreme Court has determined that the Due Process Clause contain both "substantive" and "procedural" components. Procedural due process is concerned with fairness of the procedures employed when the government seeks to deprive an individual of their property interests. The substantive component "bars certain arbitrary, wrongful government actions 'regardless of the fairness of the procedures used to implement them.'" The substantive due process inquiry revolves around deprivation of a person's property is justified.

The District Court Judge Lin have deprived Golden of his property without due process of law, and has denied Golden, a Black and/or African American, his Seventh Amendment right to a jury trial. Plus, the District Court Judge Lin lack the ability to be impartial and unbiased; and has violated certain codes of conduct for United States Judges:

> Canon 2A. "An appearance of impropriety occurs when reasonable minds, with knowledge of all the relevant circumstances disclosed by a reasonable inquiry, would conclude that the judge's honesty, integrity, impartiality, temperament, or fitness to serve as a judge is impaired."
>
> "[P]ublic manifestation by a judge of the judge's knowing approval of invidious discrimination on any basis gives the appearance of impropriety under Canon 2 and diminishes [] the integrity and impartiality of the judiciary, in violation of Canon 2A."
>
> "The duty under Canon 2 to act in a manner that promotes public confidence in the integrity and impartiality of the judiciary applies to all the judge's activities, including the discharge of the judge's adjudicative [] responsibilities. The duty to be respectful includes [] avoid [] behavior that could reasonably be interpreted as [], prejudice or bias."

> Canon 3C. "Disqualification. (1) A judge shall disqualify himself or herself in a proceeding in which the judge's impartiality might reasonably be questioned, including []: (a) the judge has a personal bias or prejudice concerning a party..."

> Canon 3B(6). "Public confidence in the integrity and impartiality of the judiciary is promoted when judges take appropriate action based on reliable information of likely misconduct. Appropriate action [] should be to prevent harm to those affected by the misconduct and to prevent recurrence."

As Justice Kennedy acknowledged in *Williams v. Pennsylvania,* impartiality in our justice system and the guarantees of due process are "necessary to the public legitimacy of judicial pronouncements and to the rule of law itself."

The Northern District of California Court Joins the Conspiracy

The Northern District of California Court, who is bound by and must follow the decisions of the U.S. Court of Appeals for the Federal Circuit [vertical stare decisis] fail to abide by the Circuit's decision in *Larry Golden v. Google LLC* Case No. 22-1267, that a "smartphone" [Qualcomm's Smartphone for Snapdragon Insiders] literally and/or under the doctrine of equivalents infringes Golden's "independent claims from U.S. Patent Nos. 10,163,287, 9,589,439, and 9,069,189 ... and it does so in a relatively straightforward manner". The District Court denied Golden [systemic/structural racism] a trial by jury in this patent infringement claim that is an issue-of-fact [U.S. CONST. amend. VII].

Likewise, the U.S. Court of Appeals for the Federal Circuit [horizontal stare decisis] fail to adhere to the Circuit's own precedence in *Larry Golden v. Google LLC* Case No. 22-1267, that a "smartphone" [Qualcomm's Smartphone for Snapdragon Insiders] literally and/or under the doctrine of equivalents infringes Golden's independent claims from U.S. Patent Nos. 10,163,287, 9,589,439, and 9,069,189 ... "and it does so in a relatively straightforward manner". The Appellate Court was complicit in denying Golden, a Black and/or African American, [systemic/structural racism] a trial by jury in this patent infringement claim that is an issue-of-fact [U.S. CONST. amend. VII].

The District Court and the Appellate Court ignored the precedence set by the U.S. Court of Appeals for the Federal Circuit [vertical stare decisis] in *Larry Golden v. Google LLC* Case No. 22-1267 that establishes the "smartphone" directly infringes at least Golden's independent claims from U.S. Patent Nos. 10,163,287, 9,589,439, and 9,069,189 ... "and it does so in a relatively straightforward manner", when establishing the "direct infringement" requirement for induced patent infringement—35 U.S.C. § 271(b); and, contributory patent infringement—35 U.S.C. § 271(c).

The District Court and the Appellate Court fail to realize it is a jury's responsibility to decide if Qualcomm, with knowledge, has induced patent infringement by selling its Qualcomm Snapdragon Chipset that "ties" Golden's patented CPUs, through advertising; with instructions; and with a threat to refuse licensing its cellular modems for smartphones if the OEMs (i.e., Samsung; Google) does not purchase the two combined components [Golden's patented CPUs and Qualcomm's patented cellular modems] that forms Qualcomm's Snapdragon Chipset/SoC/CPU/Processor [*FTC. v. Qualcomm,* 411 F. Supp. 3d 658 (N.D. Cal. 2019).]

The District Court and the Appellate Court fail to realize it is a jury's responsibility to decide if Qualcomm, with knowledge, has offered to sell or has sold within the United States, Qualcomm's Snapdragon Chipset that "ties" Golden's patented CPUs [*FTC. v. Qualcomm*]; is liable as a contributory infringer for using the "chipset" in practicing Golden's patented process, constituting a material part of the Golden's smartphone invention, knowing the same to be especially made or especially adapted for use in an infringement of Golden's patent(s), and not a staple article or commodity of commerce suitable for substantial non infringing use [contributory infringement].

The District Court and the Appellate Court ignored the precedence set by the U.S. Court of Appeals for the Federal Circuit [vertical stare decisis] in *Eko Brands, LLC v. Adrian Rivera Maynez Enters., Inc.*, 946 F.3d 1367 (Fed. Cir. 2020); "[t]he Federal Circuit court emphasized the actual standard that "willfulness requires a jury [U.S. CONST. amend. VII] to find no more than deliberate or intentional infringement."

On November 4, 2010, Golden emailed Kate Lane, Strategic IP, Qualcomm Incorporated (E-mail: clane@qualcomm.com); Direct: (858-658-2047)), to inform Ms. Lane of certain patented technology (i.e., CMDC—Smartphone—device; central processing unit (CPU)), and asked if Qualcomm would be interested in entering into a licensing agreement. December 7, 2010, Golden mailed letters addressed to the attention of

Qualcomm's Chairman & CEO Dr. Paul E. Jacobs and Qualcomm's EVP & President Derek Aberle, informing the Executives of the Patent Owner's (Golden) patented technology and asked if Qualcomm would be interested in entering into a licensing agreement. After 10 months, Ms. Lane responded back via e-mail on September 29, 2011 with, "Hi Larry, I'm just checking in to see if this portfolio is still available for purchase. Please let me know. Thank you, Kate". On October 5, 2011, Ms. Lane responded via e-mail, "Thanks Larry, [c]an you please take a few moments to fill out the attached Patent Information Request form for this? Please let me know if you have any questions. Best regards, Kate". On October 11, 2011, the Patent Owner (Golden) returned via e-mail, the answered Patent Information Request form to Ms. Lane. The Patent Owner made several attempts to contact Ms. Lane via e-mail and by phone after that, but never heard back from Ms. Lane. This evidence allows Golden to argue to a jury [U.S. CONST. amend. VII] that his patented technology was vital to Qualcomm's chipsets and smartphone products being able to compete.

The District Court and the Appellate Court fail to realize that regardless of whether the above evidence ultimately results in a willfulness finding, getting the evidence before the jury [U.S. CONST. amend. VII] may increase the likelihood that the jury [U.S. CONST. amend. VII] will find infringement and the asserted patents valid. Depriving Golden, a Black and/or African American, of his right to present Qualcomm's alleged deliberate and intentional infringement to a jury, not only violates Golden's right granted under the Seventh

Amendment, it also demonstrates and verifies Golden's claim of racism [systemic and structural racism].

Co-Conspirator Judge Rita F. Lin Protects Qualcomm's "*DOUBLE STANDARD*"

A double standard is defined as a rule or principle which is unfairly applied in different ways to different people or groups, and is a concept that can still be heavily applied to the history of the United States. The topics of racism, discrimination, and prejudice make many individuals uncomfortable, furious, or indifferent. Since humans began developing social classes, racial division has been a key factor in how societies organize - however, it's important to note that race is simply a social construction. Clark0, Anthony. *"Double standards are stunting America's growth."* UWIRE Text, 8 May 2020, p. 1. Gale Academic OneFile, link.gale.com/ apps/doc/A623469076/AONE?u=anon~18e9207f&sid=googleScholar&xid=3bcd7ca9. Accessed 17 Aug. 2023.

Qualcomm announced it was developing the Scorpion central processing unit (CPU) for mobile devices in November 2005. This was followed by the first shipments of the Snapdragon system-on-chip product, which includes a CPU, camera support and other software and semiconductors, in November 2007.

Qualcomm is the world's biggest provider of mobile chips, and it created technology that's essential for connecting phones to cellular networks. The company derives a significant portion of its revenue from licensing those inventions to hundreds of device makers, with the fee based on the value of the phone, not the components.

Because Qualcomm owns patents related to 3G, 4G and 5G networking technology, as well as other features like *software*, all handset makers [i.e., Google] building a device that connects to cellular networks have to pay it a licensing fee, even if they don't use Qualcomm's [*software*] chips. https://www.cnet.com/tech/mobile/qualcomm-settles-huawei-patent-spat-warns-of-5g-flagship-phone-delay-likely-the-iphone/

Qualcomm receives a licensing fee on the price of handsets (i.e., smartphones) that Golden, an African American inventor, owns the patent rights for. Qualcomm receives the royalty fee even if Google don't use Qualcomm's *software* chips. Google's Pixel devices are "capable of" being modified by Qualcomm's Snapdragon X65 5G Modem-RF *software* to operate in an infringing manner is not sufficient, by itself, to support a finding of infringement." *Telemac Cellular Corp. v. Topp Telecom, Inc.*, 247 F.3d 1316, 1330 (Fed. Cir. 2001).

The Federal Circuit has applied this principle in cases involving the modification of hardware through the addition of *software*. See *Nazomi Commc'ns, Inc. v. Nokia Corp.*, 739 F.3d 1339, 1346 (Fed. Cir. 2014) (finding that the defendants' products "do not infringe without modification—the modification of installing the required software").

Based on the Federal Circuit's principles, Qualcomm should not be receiving royalties because the infringement only occurs with the *software* modification of the smartphone. Qualcomm is especially privileged because Qualcomm collects royalties on the price of the smartphone, even when the *software* modification is made by someone other than Qualcomm. Following is an image of Qualcomm's Snapdragon X65 5G Modem-RF [*software]* System and Golden's Independent Claim 1 of Golden's '189 patent asserted in this case.

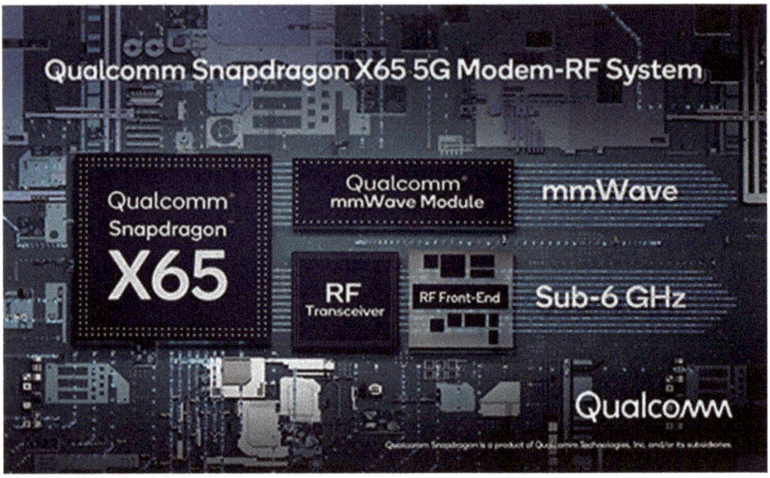

Patent #: 9,096,189; Independent Claim 1 [Asserted in Complaint]
A communication device of at least one of a cell phone, ***a smart phone***, a desktop, a handheld, a PDA, a laptop, or a computer terminal for monitoring products, interconnected to a product for communication therebetween, ***comprising***:
at least one of a central processing unit (CPU) for executing and carrying out the instructions of a computer program, a network processor which is specifically targeted at the networking application domain, or ***a front-end processor*** for communication between a host computer and other devices;

whereupon the communication device, is ***interconnected to a product equipped to receive signals from or send signals to*** lock or unlock doors, activate or deactivate security systems, activate or deactivate multi-sensor detection systems, or to activate or deactivate cell phone detection systems
wherein at least one satellite connection, Bluetooth connection, WiFi connection, internet connection, ***radio frequency (RF) connection***, cellular connection, broadband connection... ***short range radio frequency (RF) connection*** is capable of signal communication with the transmitter and the receiver of the communication device and ***transceivers*** of the products;

When Golden, an African American inventor, attempts to prove infringement in this case, Golden case is dismissed because "Google contends that "Mr. Golden thus alleges not that Google sells infringing Pixel devices, but that someone else could modify Google's Pixel devices, by adding non-Google software, to make them allegedly infringing'."

Upon information and belief, Google pays Qualcomm a royalty fee on the price of each smartphone sold if Google uses Qualcomm's software, or chose not to use Qualcomm's software; Qualcomm's infringement theory of "software modification" still stands.

Inside every cellular device [Google smartphone] is a component known as a cellular modem. Google developing its own phone processor would mean dumping the Qualcomm SoCs it usually uses. Of course, you can never truly be rid of Qualcomm: Google would presumably still need to use Qualcomm modems, something that even Apple still needs to do. There are other modem manufacturers out there—Samsung, Huawei, Mediatek—but Qualcomm's combination of patents and strong-arm licensing techniques has effectively locked its competitors out of the US and other markets.

Qualcomm's core technology connects devices — including Apple's iPhone 12 lineup — to cellular networks, and acts as the brains of phones such as Samsung's Galaxy S21 devices. It's benefitted from soaring demand for 5G chips as the tech industry moves to the newest standard of connectivity. https://www.cnet.com/roadshow/news/qualcomm-makes-cars-even-smarter-with-its-newest-snapdragon-auto-chipsets/

In stronger signal areas, the antennas can work in parallel, and the tower can simultaneously send a different signal to each antenna using the same broadcast channels. In short, Qualcomm's cellular modems do not work without the cellular towers. Which also means Qualcomm's cellular modems lacks utility and are therefore unpatentable.

Cellular technology is the most common way for RVers and Cruisers to get online - whether utilizing a smart-phone, a mobile hotspot (aka Jetpacks or MiFis), or a full-on cellular-embedded router. A modem translates analog wireless signals to/from the cell tower to your digital devices. Cellular bands are the invisible highways in the sky that the cell towers use to communicate.

Double Standard—Comparison

Qualcomm's wireless cellular modems' software is located in all of Google's Pixel smartphones. Qualcomm's wireless cellular modems must be interconnected with a cellular tower in order to function. The Qualcomm wireless cellular modem is also interconnected to the Google smartphone central processing unit (CPU) that is located inside the Google Pixel smartphone device.

According to Judge Rita F. Lin's non-infringement theory of "a third-party must modify the device in order for it to function", ***every*** patent that Qualcomm owns for its wireless cellular modems that must be modified by the third-party(s) [AT&T, Verizon, T-Mobile] are invalid because they are unenforceable. Likewise, the same results applies when Judge Rita F. Lin's theory of non-infringement "the device must be modified with software for it to function".

> The Qualcomm X62 modem is the mainstream version of the flagship X65 - and marks the beginning of 5G "Phase 2" becoming everyday technology.

Under normal conditions, both Golden and Qualcomm's patents would be considered invalid for lack of utility which makes them unenforceable, or both Golden and Qualcomm's patents would be "presumed valid" upon issue from the USPTO.

But these aren't normal conditions. Golden is a Black and/or African American inventor, and Qualcomm is a White-owned company that has a long history of stealing the ideas of others and violated antitrust laws.

Judge Rita F. Lin and the Courts theoretically invalidated Golden's patents because "the sensors are not *native* to the manufacture of the smartphones", "third-party modification in order to function", "software modification in order to function", and failure to locate the sensors inside the smartphones. Not once in sixteen (16) years has anyone ordered Qualcomm to locate the "cellular tower"; yes, cellular tower" inside the smartphone or stated the cellular tower had to be *native* to the manufacture of the smartphone.

When Judge Rita F. Lin join the conspiracy as a co-conspirator, she became also responsible for the discrimination, prejudice, racism, and bias. Judge Rita F. Lin had all opportunity to bring Qualcomm to trial because the Federal Circuit in *Larry Golden v. Google LLC* Case No. 22-1267, that a "smartphone" [Qualcomm's Smartphone for Snapdragon Insiders] literally and/or under the doctrine of equivalents infringes

Golden's "independent claims from U.S. Patent Nos. 10,163,287, 9,589,439, and 9,069,189 ... and it does so in a relatively straightforward manner",

The Circuit also stated Golden's complaint, the same complaint submitted in this case as the "original complaint", is not facially frivolous.

When Judge Rita F. Lin join the conspiracy as a co-conspirator, she knew Qualcomm is receiving a 5% running royalty on the price of each of Golden's patented smartphones [including Google], and is doing so without license or authorization.

When Judge Rita F. Lin join the conspiracy as a co-conspirator, she also knew Qualcomm is "tying" Golden's patented CPU to Qualcomm's cellular modem and selling the combination as its Snapdragon CPU/Chipset; and it also collecting a royalty on Golden's patented CPU.

Instead of bringing Golden's allegations that the Google Tensor CPU/Chipset allegedly infringes Golden's patents to a jury, Judge Rita F. Lin decided to show her loyalty to the intent of the conspiracy by protecting Qualcomm and using Golden's case against Qualcomm against him:

> Likewise, for contributory infringement, the FAC fails to plead facts supporting any of the elements of that claim against Google: "(1) selling a device capable of infringing the patent, which is not suitable for substantial non-infringing use; (2) with knowledge that the infringing device was especially adapted for use in an infringement of such patent; and (3)

actual infringement by another. ***Golden v. Qualcomm, Inc., No. 22-CV-03283-HSG, 2023 WL 2530857, at *3 (N.D. Cal. Mar. 15, 2023).*** For example, the FAC lacks factual allegations regarding Google's knowledge of the patents-in-suit and patent infringement. Also, the FAC does not explain to whose infringement the Tensor Chipset contributes, and his allegations that the Tensor Chipset lacks any substantial non-infringing uses are entirely conclusory. (See FAC at 3–4.)

Furthermore, Golden has had multiple suits with similar allegations dismissed, some as frivolous. See, e.g., Golden v. Samsung Elecs. Am., Inc., No. 23-CV-00048-WHO, 2023 WL 3919466 (N.D. Cal. June 8, 2023), aff'd, No. 2023-2120, 2024 WL 539973 (Fed. Cir. Feb. 12, 2024); ***Golden v. Qualcomm, Inc., No. 22-CV-03283-HSG, 2023 WL 2530857 (N.D. Cal. Mar. 15, 2023)*** Golden v. Apple Inc., No. 20-cv-04353-JD-KFM, 2021 WL 5074739 (D.S.C. Nov. 2, 2021) (dismissing complaint as "frivolous"); Golden v. Apple Inc., No. 20-cv-02270-JD-KFM, 2021 WL 4260782 (D.S.C. Sept. 20, 2021) (dismissing complaint as "frivolous"). As such, leave to amend is denied.

CHAPTER ELEVEN

GOLDEN ALLEGES JUDGE RITA F. LIN, WITH KNOWLEDGE, WILLFULLY VIOLATED GOLDEN'S SEVENTH AMENDMENT CONSTITUTIONAL RIGHT TO A TRIAL BY JURY.

Judge Rita F. Lin knowingly violated Golden's civil rights [42 U.S.C. section 1983] when she deprived Golden of his guaranteed constitutional right to a trial by jury under the Seventh Amendment of the United States Constitution because of his race.

No particular form for a jury trial demand is prescribed by California statute or court rule. (See Code Civ. Proc. § 631(a): "[t]he right to a trial by jury as declared by Section 16 of Article I of the California Constitution shall be preserved to the parties inviolate"; "[t]rial by jury is an inviolate right—not to be violated or broken—and shall be secured to all").

A demand may be made either in writing or orally on the record (i.e., Golden made the demand in the initial complaint at Dkt. 1; and, in the case management statement at Dkt. 34).

> [Cal. Rules of Court, rule 3.727. Subjects to be considered at the case management conference: "(13) Whether a jury trial is demanded, and, if so, the identity of each party requesting a jury trial; (14) If the trial date has not been previously set, the date by which the case will be ready for trial and the available trial dates; (15) The [] length of trial"]

It has been over twenty-five years since the Court last assessed the scope of the constitutional right to a jury in a patent-infringement case. *Markman v. Westview Instruments, Inc.*, 517 U.S. 370, 372 (1996). More remarkable, that decision has been its only direct pronouncement on the matter in the 230 years that patent infringement has been actionable [Act of Apr. 10, 1790, ch. 7, §§ 1, 4, 1 Stat. 109, 110, 111 (first federal patent act)].

The Seventh Amendment requires juries in "Suits at common law" [U.S. CONST. amend. VII]; law courts always offered juries; and early juries tried nearly all infringement and validity issues.

Patent infringement is an issue-of-fact tried by a jury under the Seventh Amendment. Typically, a jury is asked to decide whether the evidence shows that the defendant is performing the claimed invention.

Many litigants now prefer juries whenever the Constitution says they can demand them, and they always can when the patentee seeks damages at trial (with or without injunctive relief). Patent cases were "tried at law in the 18th century, and there is no dispute that infringement cases today must be tried to a jury." *Markman,* 517 U.S. at 377.

Markman, in fact, involved a patentee who sought damages and injunctive relief, the same as Golden in this current case, and yet neither the parties nor the Court thought twice in assuming that the patentee's case cleared the first step of the Court's historical test.

The Court quickly cleared the first step because the petition for review noted that the patentee [same as Golden] sought damages. Petition for a *Writ of Certiorari* at *Markman,* 517 U.S. 370 (No. 95-26), 1995 WL 17063340, ("In a patent infringement action for damages, is there a right to a jury trial under the Seventh Amendment of the United States Constitution of genuine factual disputes about the meaning of a patent?").

The Seventh Amendment uses the term "common law" to refer to cases in which the right to jury trial was preserved. The Supreme Court resolved the difficulty by stressing the fundamental nature of the jury trial right and protecting it against decrease to equitable principles.

Long-standing equity principles, according to the Court, dictated that "only under the most imperative circumstances which in view of the flexible procedures of the Federal Rules we cannot now anticipate, can the right to a jury trial of legal issues be lost through prior determination of equitable claims." Golden's right was lost through the racist and prejudicial tactics of Judge Rita F. Lin.

In *Ross v. Bernhard*, the Court held that the right to a jury trial depends on the nature of the issue to be tried, rather than the procedural framework in which it is raised. Because the Federal Rules of Civil Procedure merged law and equity in the federal courts, there was no longer any procedural obstacle to transferring jurisdiction to the law side once the equitable issue of standing was decided. Thus, the Court continued, if the claim that is asserted is legal in nature, it should be heard on the law side before a jury.

Sullivan v. Redfield, 23 F. Cas. 357 (C.C.D.N.Y. 1825) (No. 13,597), in 1825 exemplifies the early view on these issues. There, Justice Thompson stated that in cases properly filed in equity, the validity of an invention patent was something on which the parties had a right to a jury, and thus the court was obligated to send the parties to the court's law side for trial:

> "Whether the complainant's patent is good and valid so as ultimately to secure to him the right he claims, is not a question for decision upon the equity side of this court. That is a question which belongs to a court of law, in which the parties have a right of trial by a jury."

Issues of Fact are to be Determined by the Jury

The primary purpose of the Seventh Amendment is to preserve the common law distinction between the province of the court and that of the jury, whereby, in the absence of express or implied consent to the contrary, issues of law are resolved by the court and issues of fact are to be determined by the jury under appropriate instructions by the court. *Baltimore & Carolina Line v. Redman,* 295 U.S. 654, 657 (1935); *Walker v. New Mexico & So. Pac. R.R.*, 165 U.S. 593, 596 (1897); *Gasoline Products Co. v. Champlin Ref. Co.*, 283 U.S. 494, 497–99 (1931); *Dimick v. Schiedt*, 293 U.S. 474, 476, 485–86 (1935).

Patent infringement is an issue-of-fact tried by a jury under the Seventh Amendment. The issues of facts, acknowledged by the Defendant in their second motion to dismiss, are to be determined by a jury. The following issues are taken from Google's Motion to Dismiss Plaintiff's Amended Complaint, NDC Case 3:22-cv-05246-RFL Document 44 Filed 09/07/23:

- "In pleading direct patent infringement, a plaintiff cannot satisfy "the pleading standards set forth in *Twombly* and *Iqbal* 'by reciting the claim elements and merely concluding that the accused protect [sic] has those elements. There must be some factual allegations that, when taken as true, articulate why it is plausible that the accused product infringes the patent claim.'"
- "Where a plaintiff "fails to allege facts plausibly supporting an inference that [the defendant] purposely induced another party to infringe any patent," courts dismiss claims of induced infringement."

- "Willful blindness is a high standard, requiring that the alleged inducer (1) subjectively believe that there is a high probability that a fact exists and (2) take deliberate actions to avoid learning of that fact."

- "[P]utting Global-Tech together with *Iqbal,* the question before the Court" at the pleading stage is whether a plaintiff has pleaded "sufficient facts . . . for the Court to infer" willful blindness."

- "The amended complaint contains no allegations either that Google "subjectively believe[d] that there is a high probability that a fact exists" or that Google took any "deliberate actions to avoid learning of that fact."

- "Mr. Golden merely asserts that Google contributes its Google Tensor Chipset, but does not allege to whom Google contributes the Tensor Chipset, nor any factual allegations supporting his threadbare claims that Google is liable for contributory infringement"

- "Here, just as in Bill of Lading, the complaint "supplies the very facts which defeat its claims of contributory infringement."

- "To state a claim for willful infringement, the plaintiff must plead that the defendant acted with knowledge of the patent and of his alleged infringement, or equivalent facts." ... "Although the jury decides willfulness, willfulness only goes to the jury if it was properly framed by the pleadings."

A patent infringement claim is an issue-of-fact tried by a jury under the Seventh Amendment. The issues of facts, acknowledged by the Defendant in their second motion to dismiss, are to be decided by a jury. Judge Rita F. Lin joined the conspiracy as a co-conspirator and dismissed Golden's case because he's a Black and/or African American who brought a case of stealing against the White-owned company Google, in her Court that is governed and guided by systemic and structural racism.

Judge Rita F. Lin's racism is so deep she is willing, with knowledge, to violate Golden's Constitutional rights under the Fifth Amendment Clause of the U.S. Constitution ("deprivation of property without due process of law, and without paying just compensation"), and the Seventh Amendment of the U.S. Constitution ("guaranteed right to a trial by jury in claims of patent infringement, that are issues-of-fact").

A jury needs to decide if the phases "smartphone must be modified for detection functionality", "modified by a third-party in order to function", and "software modification is needed for infringement to occur". Judge Rita F. Lin improperly added these abstract ideas.

The three phases are theoretical or hypothetical, and are not found in any of Golden's patent claim limitations asserted in this case.

> In *Research Corporation Technologies Inc. v. Microsoft Corp.*, 627 F.3d 859 (Fed. Cir. 2010) (RCT). The patent at issue was U.S. Patent No. 5,111,310. Hypothetical claims 1-3 are directed to an abstract idea [ineligible] and have additional elements that amount to significantly more than the abstract

idea because they show an improvement in the functioning of the computer itself and also show an improvement to another technology/technical field, either of which can show eligibility.

In *SiRF Technology Inc. v. International Trade Commission*, 601 F.3d 1319 (Fed. Cir. 2010) (SiRF Tech). The patent at issue was U.S. Patent No. 6,417,801. Hypothetical claims 1 and 2 are directed to an abstract idea [ineligible] and have additional elements that amount to significantly more than the abstract idea because they show an improvement to another technology or technical field.

In *Google Inc. v. Simpleair, Inc.*, Covered Business Method Case No. CBM 2014-00170 (Jan. 22, 2015), ... The patent at issue was U.S. Patent No. 7,035,914 entitled "*System and Method for Transmission of Data.*" Hypothetical claim 1 is directed to an abstract idea [ineligible] and does not have additional elements that amount to significantly more than the abstract idea. Hypothetical claim 2 also recites an abstract idea [ineligible] but does contain additional elements that amount to significantly more because there are meaningful limitations beyond generally linking the use of the abstract idea to a particular technological environment.

The following claim was found ineligible by the Federal Circuit in *buySAFE, Inc. v. Google, Inc.*, 765 F.3d 1350 (Fed. Cir. 2014). The patent at issue was U.S. Patent No. 7,644,019. The claim is directed to an abstract idea and has additional elements that do not amount to significantly more than the abstract idea.

For the same reasons set forth above, by taking all the abstract ideas and adding them to the claim elements individually, and in combination; Golden's patent claims as a whole amounts to significantly more than the abstract ideas of "smartphone must be modified for detection functionality", "modified by a third-party in order to function", and "software modification is needed for infringement to occur".

Upon reviewing the chart below, it's obvious Judge Rita F. Lin does not know what she's talking about. Nowhere in the claim limitations are the phases "smartphone must be modified for detection functionality", "modified by a third-party in order to function", and "software modification is needed for infringement to occur".

Google Pixel 5 Smartphone	**Patent #: 10,163,287; Independent Claim 5**	**Patent #: 9,589,439; Indep. Claim 23**	**Patent #: 9,096,189; Independent Claim 1**
	A monitoring device, comprising:	A cell phone comprising:	A communication device of at least one of a cell phone, a smart phone, a desktop, a handheld, a PDA, a laptop, or a computer terminal ...

CPU: Octa-core (1 × 2.4 GHz Kryo 475 Prime & 1 × 2.2 GHz Kryo 475 Gold & 6 × 1.8 GHz Kryo 475 Silver) System-on-a-chip: Qualcomm Snapdragon 765G	at least one central processing unit (CPU);	a central processing unit (CPU) for executing and carrying out the instructions of a computer program;	at least one of a central processing unit (CPU) for executing and carrying out the instructions of a computer program, ...
Android Team Awareness Kit, ATAK (built on the Android operating system) is a digital application available to warfighters throughout the DoD. ATAK—end-user device smartphone or tablet. With DTRA's contribution, ATAK now includes ... (CBRN) plug-ins.	one or more detectors in communication with the at least one CPU for detecting at least one of chemical, biological, radiological, or explosive agents	at least one of a chemical sensor, a biological sensor, an explosive sensor, a human sensor, a contraband sensor, or a radiological sensor capable of being disposed within, on, upon or adjacent the cell phone;	wherein the communication device receives a signal via any of one or more products listed in any of the plurality of product grouping categories;
Android Team Awareness Kit, ATAK (built on the Android operating system) provides a single	at least one of a transmitter or a transceiver in communication with ... CPU...	whereupon a signal sent to the receiver ... causes a signal that includes at least	whereupon the communication device, is interconnected to a product equipped to

interface for viewing and controlling different CBRN-sensing tech.		one of location data ...	receive signals from or send signals to...

After reviewing the chart, it's easy to see Golden's only responsibility is to first identify the Google Pixel smartphone as "[a] monitoring device", "[a] cell phone", and "[a] communication device". Next, Golden needs to identify where in the Google smartphone the central processing unit(s) (CPUs) can be found. Following, Golden needs to identify where in the Google smartphone the CBRNE are found, or identify the CBRNE detectors/sensors that are disposed within, on, upon or adjacent the cell phone. Lastly, Golden needs to identify where in the Google smartphone the transmitters, receivers, and transceivers.

A claim construction hearing is also needed so that Judge Rita F. Lin can identify and explain "software modification". It's important Judge Lin identify and point to what third-party is using what software, to modify what device. Judge Lin's language is so broad it's hard to pin point exactly what she is saying.

For example: The DTRA ATAK software is built on the Google Android Open-Source Operating system software; the Google Android Open-Source Operating System [software] that is built on the open-source code of Linux; the Linux Operating System is a type of operating system that is built upon the Linux Kernel; and Linux distribution is an operating system that is made up of a collection of software based on Linux kernel. Therefore, again, what software, what third-party, what device? Because, through it all the operating systems and the third-party devices are interconnected to Golden's patented central processing unit for functionality.

The only time Golden is responsibility for locating a third-party, or software in the Google smartphone; and locating in the Google smartphone the unforeseen abstract step of modifying, is when Judge Rita F. Lin orders Golden to do so. That's why a trial by jury is not only a right guaranteed Golden by the Seventh Amendment of the United States Constitution, in this case a jury trial is pertinent to the pursuit for justice and fairness.

CONCLUSION

In *Twombly*, the Supreme Court considered the adequacy of a complaint alleging that defendants orchestrated an antitrust conspiracy in violation of the Sherman Act. 550 U.S. at 555. The Court observed that the complaint contained no factual allegations of an agreement as needed to establish a conspiracy. *Id.* at 564. Instead, the pleading rested on legal conclusions premised upon descriptions of parallel conduct. *Id. Twombly* held that Rule 8 requires plaintiffs to include enough facts "to raise a right to relief above a speculative level," and cautioned that "a formulaic recitation of the elements of a cause of action will not do." *Id.* at 555.

The Supreme Court provided further clarification of the necessary pleading standard in *Iqbal,* where it considered a claim alleging that several high-ranking officials violated the First and Fifth Amendments by purposefully instituting a policy of discrimination that resulted in plaintiff's incarceration at a facility where the conditions of confinement were inadequate. 556 U.S. at 668–69. *Iqbal* explained that "[t]wo working principles underlie" *Twombly*: (1) courts need not accept as true legal conclusions or "[t]hreadbare recitals of the elements of a cause of action, supported by mere conclusory statements;" and (2) only a complaint that states a plausible claim for relief with well pleaded facts demonstrating the pleader's entitlement to relief can survive a motion to dismiss. Id. at 678–79. Because the complaint in *Iqbal* included only conclusory assertions of discrimination without factual allegations that plausibly gave rise to an entitlement of relief, the complaint was fatally defective. *Id.* at 679–80. The Court explained that plaintiff's allegation that officials "purposefully adopted" a policy of discrimination was inadequate because it lacked factual allegations that could "'nudg[e]' [his] claim of purposeful discrimination 'across the line from conceivable to plausible.'" *Id.* at 682–83 (quoting *Twombly*, 550 U.S. at 570).

Taken together, *Iqbal* and *Twombly* require well-pleaded facts, not legal conclusions, *Twombly*, 550 U.S. at 570, that "plausibly give rise to an entitlement to relief," *Iqbal*, 556 U.S. at 679. The plausibility of a pleading thus derives from its well-pleaded factual allegations. *Id*

The Federal Circuit on 09/08/2022, in *Larry Golden v. Google LLC*; Case No. 22-1267 — "VACATED AND REMANDED" the relevant Case No: 22-1267 Document 15; back to the District Court "to be filed and request service of process". The Federal Circuit determined the complaint, "includes a detailed claim chart mapping features of an accused product, the Google Pixel 5 Smartphone, to independent claims from U.S. Patent Nos. 10,163,287, 9,589,439, and 9,069,189" ... "in a relatively straightforward manner" ... and that the [Circuit] "express no opinion as to the adequacy of the complaint or claim chart except that it is not facially frivolous."

> In a Three-Judge Panel DISCUSSION: "Under the pleading standards set forth in *Bell Atlantic Corp. v. Twombly*, 550 U.S.

544 (2007), and *Ashcroft v. Iqbal,* 556 U.S. 662 (2009), a court must dismiss a complaint if it fails to allege "enough facts to state a claim to relief that is plausible on its face." *Twombly,* 550 U.S. at 570 ... [T]his standard "requires more than labels and conclusions, and a formulaic recitation of the elements of a cause of action will not do." *Id.* at 555 (citation omitted). A plaintiff must allege facts that give rise to "more than a sheer possibility that a defendant has acted unlawfully." *Iqbal,* 556 U.S. at 678 (citation omitted) ... this court has explained that a plaintiff ... must plead "'enough fact[s] to raise a reasonable expectation that discovery will reveal' that the defendant is liable for the misconduct alleged."

"Mr. Golden's complaint includes a detailed claim chart mapping features of an accused product, the Google Pixel 5 Smartphone, to independent claims from U.S. Patent Nos. 10,163,287, 9,589,439, and 9,069,189 ... It [claim chart] attempts [] to map claim limitations to infringing product features, and it does so in a relatively straightforward manner ...[W]e conclude that the district court's decision in the Google case is not correct with respect to at least the three claims mapped out in the claim chart. Mr. Golden has made efforts to identify exactly how the accused products meet the limitations of his claims in this chart...."

In the Federal Circuit's order to vacate and remand, the Circuit determined Golden's complaint is not facially frivolous; has alleged enough facts to state a claim to relief that is plausible on its face; has plead 'enough fact[s] to raise a reasonable expectation that discovery will reveal' that the defendant is liable for the misconduct alleged; has plead facts that give rise to more than a sheer possibility that a defendant has acted unlawfully; has included a detailed claim chart mapping features of an accused product, the Google Pixel 5 Smartphone, to independent claims from U.S. Patent Nos. 10,163,287, 9,589,439, and 9,069,189; attempts [] to map claim limitations to infringing product features, and it does so in a relatively straightforward manner; and, has made efforts to identify exactly how the accused products meet the limitations of his claims in this chart.

The Federal Circuit "conclude[d] that the district court's decision in the Google case is not correct with respect to at least the three claims mapped out in the claim chart." Which means Golden submitted enough factual information on literal infringement, infringement under the doctrine of equivalents, induced infringement, contributory infringement, willful infringement, and joint infringement; to Judge Rita F. Lin in this Northern District of California Court case.

The question here is, what motivated Judge Rita F. Lin to overturn every cause of action [above] Golden submitted against Google, that was identical to the cause of actions submitted to the Federal Circuit?

Judge Rita F. Lin overstepped the doctrine of *vertical stare decisis* to overturn every cause of action, and she did so without a jury; without discovery; and without claim construction. Judge Lin's motivation stems from racism and the conspiracies she joined as a co-conspirator.

Vertical stare decisis

Vertical stare decisis binds Judge Rita F. Lin to follow strictly the decisions of higher courts within the same jurisdiction (e.g., the Northern District of California Court must follow the decisions of the U.S. Court of Appeals for the Federal Circuit). The Supreme Court defines vertical stare decisis as the doctrine, "a lower court [Judge Rita F. Lin] must strictly follow the decision(s) handed down by a higher court within the same jurisdiction".

Judge Rita F. Lin engages in vertical stare decisis when she applies precedent from the higher court. For example, if the Northern District of California Court [Judge Rita F. Lin] adhered to a previous ruling from the United States Court of Appeals for the Federal Circuit, in *Larry Golden v. Google LLC*; Case No. 22-1267, that would be vertical stare decisis.

When Judge Rita F. Lin applies the decision from the higher court, [vertical stare decisis] it bars Google from challenging whether Golden has pled enough facts and provided sufficient notice to the Defendant Google. The Federal Circuit's ruling: "the complaint includes a detailed claim chart mapping features of an accused product, the Google [] Smartphone, to independent claims from U.S. Patent Nos. 10,163,287, 9,589,439, and 9,069,189" … 'in a relatively straightforward manner'", indicates Golden has pled enough facts and any challenges Judge Rita F. Lin allows should be presented to a jury.

Again, Golden believes Judge Lin's motivation to disregard the decisions of the higher court, stem from racism and the conspiracies she joined as a co-conspirator.

"Due Process"

The Fifth Amendment states, "No person shall...be deprived of life, liberty, or property, without due process of law;", and among other things, the government and Senior Judge Bruggink cannot deprive Golden of his property without following certain procedures. This is known as "due process," which is further broken down into two concepts: procedural due process and substantive due process.

The Supreme Court has explained that [p]procedural due process rules are meant to protect persons [Golden] not from the deprivation, but from the mistaken [unfair] or unjustified deprivation of his property. *Carey v. Piphus*, 435 U.S. 247, 259 (1978).

As the Supreme Court summed up in *James v. Campbell*, 104 U.S. 356, 358 (1882), a case concerning the alleged appropriation of a patent by the Government:

> "[A patent] confers upon the patentee an exclusive property in the patented invention which cannot be appropriated or used by the government itself, without just compensation, any more than it can appropriate or use without compensation land which has been patented to a private purchaser."

Over the course of years, Senior Judge Bruggink, in multiple cases, to include this current case, has deprived Golden of his property through unfair and unjustified means that resulted in the loss of his property and the continued appropriation or use by the government without paying Golden just compensation.

Judge Rita F. Lin's procedural due process violation under the Fifth Amendment Clause of the United States Constitution is a violation of Golden's civil rights when the offense is motivated by racial discrimination.

12(b)(6)

When deciding a motion to dismiss under Rule 12(b)(6), Judge Rita F. Lin must accept as true all factual allegations in the complaint [which means all factual evidence of literal infringement determined by the Federal Circuit in *Larry Golden v. Google LLC*; Case No. 22-1267, and must draw inferences in a light most favorable to the Golden. *See Scheuer v. Rhodes*, 416 U.S. 232, 236 (1974).

"The function of a motion to dismiss is 'merely to assess the legal feasibility of the complaint, not to assay [examine] the weight of the evidence which might be offered in support thereof.'" *Mytych v. May Dept. Store Co.*, 34 F. Supp. 2d 130, 131 (D. Conn. 1999) (quoting *Ryder Energy Distribution v. Merrill Lynch Commodities, Inc.*, 748 F.2d 774, 779 (2d Cir. 1984)), and certainly not to do everything, including lying, avoiding the issues, and adjudicating outside the Court's jurisdiction, to overturn the decision of the higher United States Court of Appeals for the Federal Circuit in *Larry Golden v. Google LLC*; Case No. 22-1267.

"The issue on a motion to dismiss is not whether the Golden will prevail, but whether Golden is entitled to offer evidence to support his claims." *United States v. Yale New Haven Hosp.*, 727 F. Supp 784, 786 (D. Conn. 1990) (citing *Scheuer*, 416 U.S. at 232).

Doctrine of *Res Judicata*

The doctrine of res judicata seeks "(1) to promote judicial economy by minimizing repetitive litigation; (2) to prevent inconsistent judgments which undermine the integrity of the judicial system; and (3) to provide repose by preventing a person from being harassed by vexatious litigation." *See State v. Ellis,* 466, 497 A.2d at 990

Judge Rita F. Lin's theories of "issue preclusion" does not apply and is inapplicable to valid claims submitted with valid patents under § 271. Golden has the right to bring an action against Google for the recovery of damages any time Google appropriates or uses Golden's patented invention(s) without license or legal right to do so.

Judge Rita F. Lin's theories of jurisdiction and the boundaries the Judge applies to ***"whoever"*** under § 271(a)(b)(c), if allowed to stand, rewrites patent infringement under 35 U.S.C. § 271(a)(b)(c). Judge Rita F. Lin's non-infringement theories create "loopholes" for Google to infringe Golden's patents without liability:

Judge Rita F. Lin's non-infringement theories are displaced and only applies to a certain race of people; only at certain times; only under certain conditions; and only without using the same patents that are within the patents 20-year term limit.

It's dinosaur judges like Judge Rita F. Lin's that keeps systemic and structural racism alive in the Federal judicial system. It's obvious Golden's cases means more to Judge Rita F. Lin's than just adjudicating the merits.

It means not allowing a Black man to succeed in defending his property within her jurisdiction, and outside her jurisdiction.

Golden believes Judge Rita F. Lin's non-infringement theories are racially motivated. Golden believes Judge Rita F. Lin knew she was barred [precluded] from re-litigating the same issues of literal infringement and/or infringement under the doctrine of equivalents that had already been decided in *Larry Golden v. Google LLC*; Case No. 22-1267 with the use of identical patents and patent claims.

This document is a combined statement of facts and supporting evidence that Judge Rita F. Lin knowingly, willfully, and repeatedly violated Golden's civil rights.

Larry Golden, *Pro Se* Complainant

740 Woodruff Rd., #1102

Greenville, SC 29607

(H) 8642885605

(M) 8649927104

Email: atpg-tech@charter.net

www.ingramcontent.com/pod-product-compliance
Lightning Source LLC
LaVergne TN
LVHW050912210926
848482LV00012B/417